BOLLINGEN SERIES LXI · 2

ESSAYS OF ERICH NEUMANN

VOLUME 2

Editorial Committee

Renée Brand
William McGuire
Julie Neumann

PUBLISHED IN JOINT SPONSORSHIP WITH THE
C. G. JUNG INSTITUTE OF SAN FRANCISCO

ERICH NEUMANN

Creative Man

FIVE ESSAYS

Translated from the German by
Eugene Rolfe

BOLLINGEN SERIES LXI · 2

PRINCETON UNIVERSITY PRESS
Princeton and Oxford

Published by Princeton University Press
41 William Street, Princeton, New Jersey 08540
99 Banbury Road, Oxford OX2 6JX

press.princeton.edu

GPSR Authorized Representative: Easy Access System Europe -
Mustamäe tee 50, 10621 Tallinn, Estonia, gpsr.requests@easproject.com

This translation first published in 1979
New cloth, paperback, and e-book Bollingen Recollections editions, 2026

Cloth ISBN 9780691279152
Paperback ISBN 9780691279169
ISBN (e-book) 9780691279176

This is the second volume of number sixty-one in a series of works
sponsored by and published for Bollingen Foundation

The Library of Congress has cataloged a prior edition of this book as
follows:

Neumann, Erich.
  Creative man.

  (Essays of Erich Neumann; v. 2) (Bollingen series; 61:2)
A translation of one of the essays in the author's Der schopferische
Mensch and four other essays first published in various German
magazines.
  Includes index.
  CONTENTS: Adler, G. On Erich Neumann, 1905-1960.—Works by
Erich Neumann translated into English.—Kafka's "The trial." — [etc.]

I. Creation (Literary, artistic, etc.) —Addresses, essays, lectures.
2. Subconsciousness—Addresses essays, lectures. I. Title. II. Series:
Neumann, Erich. Essays of Erich Neumann; v. 2. III. Series: Bollingen
series; 61:2.
BF408.N37   150.19'5'0926   79-16711
ISBN 0-691-09944-8

CONTENTS

LIST OF PLATES

Following page 124. From etchings by Marc Chagall in vol. VIII, nos. 33/34, published by Editions Verve in 1956, with the title *La Bible illustrée by Marc Chagall.*

EDITORIAL NOTE

The present volume is a sequel to a volume of Neumann's essays in translation, *Art and the Creative Unconscious*, published in 1959, during his lifetime. From the body of shorter writings not previously translated into English, the editors propose to form several additional selections of essays on the model of the 1959 volume.

The title, *Creative Man*, is that of the collection *Der Schöpferische Mensch*, published in Zurich (Rhein-Verlag) also in 1959. In it Neumann published for the first time "Georg Trakl—Person und Mythos," an essay whose aim was to illuminate creative existence by a concrete example. The other four essays in that volume, more general and theoretical in their application, were all originally given as Eranos lectures and expanded for republication; they will be translated in another volume.

Three short papers, on Jung, Freud, and Chagall, respectively, were first published in the German review *Merkur* in 1955, 1957, and 1958. The essay on Freud was previously published in a translation by Eva Metman in the *Journal of Analytical Psychology*, 1956, and in *Spring*, 1957. That translation is here republished with considerable revision.

Neumann wrote commentaries on various of Kafka's writings in 1932, at a time when Kafka's work was still little known and before Neumann's first meeting with

Jung. Julie Neumann has stated: "As so much had been published on the subject in the meantime (up to the 1950s), he felt the need to become acquainted with at least some of the new work before he published his own commentaries. He was never able to carry out his plan. The one exception was the contribution that he prepared for *Geist und Werk* (1958)." That was a Festschrift for the seventy-fifth birthday of Dr. Daniel Brody, the founder of the Rhein-Verlag and publisher of the *Eranos Jahrbücher*, Neumann's *Die grosse Mutter*, and related works. To it Neumann contributed the commentary he called "The Cathedral Chapter," Part Two of the opening work in the present volume. Both our Parts One and Two were published in 1974 in the German journal *Analytische Psychologie*. Neumann in 1958 entitled his work "From the First Part of the Kafka Commentary: The Court"; we have instead used Kafka's title, *The Trial*, and have given the title "The Court" to Part One.

The prefatory article on Erich Neumann by Gerhard Adler was originally published in *Spring*, 1961. Dr. Adler, who was Neumann's close friend and the literary executor of his publications in English, has revised and slightly expanded it. His counsel in the preparation of the present volume is acknowledged with thanks.

The assistance of Wayne K. Detloff, M.D., Stanford Drew, Shändel Parks, and Virginia Detloff's work of preparing the index, are much appreciated.

For permission to quote, acknowledgment is gratefully made as follows: for quotations from Georg Trakl's poems, to Michael Hamburger and Christopher Middleton, and to Jonathan Cape Ltd., publishers of *Selected*

EDITORIAL NOTE

Poems, edited by Christopher Middleton; and to Alfred
A. Knopf, Inc., Schocken Books Inc., and Martin Secker
and Warburg Ltd., for quotations from *The Trial,* by
Franz Kafka, Definitive Edition, Revised, translated by
Willa and Edwin Muir, copyright 1937, © 1956, and
renewed 1965 by Alfred A. Knopf, Inc. Acknowledgment is also made, with appreciation, to M. Tériade for
his kindness in permitting the reproduction of Chagall's
etchings from *Verve.*

ON ERICH NEUMANN: 1905-1960

Erich Neumann died on November 5, 1960, in Tel Aviv. The news of his death—forewarned though I had been when I saw him in London only three weeks before— seemed inconceivable. So powerful was his mind, so inexhaustible seemed the reserves of his personality, so warm and generous his friendship, that it just did not seem possible that all this vitality and creativeness should have so suddenly come to an end.

I had been associated with Erich Neumann in a friendship of nearly forty years, dating back to our early student days in Germany. Even then, as a student and a young man, his creative personality asserted itself. We belonged to a circle of friends who were deeply interested in all the problems of life for which Germany after the First World War was a focal point: among them, philosophy, psychology, the Jewish question and, last but not least, poetry and art. How many nights did we not spend in intense and endless discussions on every possible aspect of existence! And there was no aspect to which the depth and width of Neumann's approach together with his passionate nature did not contribute some original and creative answer.

Poetry and art: to many it will come as a surprise to hear that Erich Neumann's first creative works were a long novel, *Der Anfang* (*The Beginning*)—a story, as we would now say, of *nigredo* and individuation, one

chapter of which was published in Germany in 1932—
and many beautiful poems. Even then he was interested
in the creative process; another of his early writings
(1933) was a commentary on the novels of Franz Kafka,
at that time still relatively unknown. His interest in
poetry and art sprang from a profoundly artistic temperament; his two last books in English, *Art and the
Creative Unconscious* and *The Archetypal World of
Henry Moore*, are witnesses of his creative participation
in the artistic process. There are also various other essays on art and poetry that have not yet appeared in
English; their publication is now projected.

The other pole of his creativity was Judaism: without
being in any way orthodox, he had his deepest roots in
the Jewish heritage, particularly its mystical side. He was
strongly influenced in his outlook by Hasidism, the great
eighteenth-century continuation of cabalistic thought.
Long before the advent of Hitler, Neumann felt strongly
related to the renewal of Jewish life in Israel (then
Palestine), so that his emigration in 1934 to Tel Aviv
was far from being forced on him by external political
circumstances. To him Israel became a true home, and
he never regretted his decision to settle so far away from
the centers of European learning. Furthermore, a great
deal of his early work was devoted to problems of Jewish
psychology. His dissertation for the degree of doctor of
philosophy[1] was on a mystical philosopher of the eight-

---

1. Diss., U. of Erlangen, 1927: "Johann Arnold Kanne: Ein
Beitrag zur Geschichte der mystischen Sprachphilosophie"; published the same year in Berlin, with the subtitle "Ein verges-
sener Romantiker."

eenth and nineteenth centuries who, a Christian, had
been profoundly influenced by Jewish esoteric thought.
There exists also a beautiful interpretation of the Jacob
and Esau myth from the early thirties, which he never
published because it seemed to him still incomplete.

Although his early studies had been focused on philosophy, he soon became more and more interested in
psychology. It was characteristic of his thoroughness
and his vitality that, once he had decided to take up psychology as a profession, he started medical training,
which he finished in 1933. It was this that prepared him
for his crucial encounter with C. G. Jung in 1934, prior
to his emigration to Palestine. Here, in Jung's approach,
he found the dynamic focus of his various interests and
gifts. Analytical psychology provided the instrument
that helped him to translate his creative insight into
practical work with other people, and for them. It was
a meeting of the greatest importance: the results of
Erich Neumann's relationship with Jung are by now
part of the history of analytical psychology.

Had it not been for the intervening years of the war,
we would have heard much earlier of Erich Neumann's
work. He utilized these years of enforced isolation for
a great variety of studies which, after the war, blossomed
into an enormous burst of creative activity. In 1947 he
visited Europe again for the first time. My family had
rented a summer house in Ascona, where we all met
and where I had the good fortune to introduce him to
Olga Froebe-Kapteyn. This meeting started a most fruitful collaboration between the two: as early as 1948 Erich
Neumann gave his first Eranos lecture, "Der Mystische

Mensch" ("Mystical Man"), and he returned every year, soon becoming one of the most important figures at Eranos. His thirteen papers published in the *Eranos Jahrbuch* show the continuous progress of his thought; lectures like the one "On the Moon and Matriarchal Consciousness" or "The Psyche and the Transformation of the Planes of Reality" opened up new psychological vistas.

We cannot evaluate his work here. But a glance at the various titles is sufficient to give an idea of the scope of his creative genius. In 1949 his first published book, *Depth Psychology and a New Ethic* (tr. 1969), showed the impact which the idea of psychological wholeness had made on a deeply ethical person. To him, self-realization seemed to impose a new ethical outlook and an obligation beyond all conventional ethical concepts. The same year saw the publication of his first great book, *The Origins and History of Consciousness* (tr. 1954), a landmark in analytical psychology. This book—with its bold scheme to illustrate the phases in the development of human consciousness by the interpretation of basic mythologems—put him immediately in the forefront of analytical psychologists. For a number of years his interest in feminine psychology became more and more the focus of his attention. "On the Moon and Matriarchal Consciousness" and his lecture to the Zurich Psychology Club that same year on "The Psychology of the Feminine" were followed in 1952 by his graceful commentary, *Amor and Psyche* (tr. 1956) and in 1955 by his second outstanding work, *The Great Mother*. Later essays are contained in *Art and the Creative Unconscious* and *The*

Archetypal World of Henry Moore, both published in 1959; in these, his interests in feminine psychology and creative art are beautifully blended. Along with his lectures at Eranos there went a continuous activity as a lecturer: in Switzerland where he became a patron of the C. G. Jung Institute, in the Netherlands, in Germany, and most of all in his beloved Israel, where he conducted regular seminars and started a group of Jungian psychologists. Numerous articles in a variety of journals show the range of his mind, and his lecture at the First International Congress of Analytical Psychology (Zurich, 1958) supplied a program for future research by building a bridge between the personalistic genetic view and the transpersonal archetypal aspects of the psyche.

Erich Neumann was the one truly creative spirit among the second generation of Jung's pupils, the only one who seemed destined to build on Jung's work and to continue it. This was, I feel, due not only to his fertile and inexhaustible mind, but to the fact that his work did not spring from his intellect but from a deep and living contact with the unconscious sources of creativity. To him, working on his unconscious material was a regular and indispensable part of life; if he did not spend the evenings and nights of his over-full working days in writing, he would give them to active imagination and to the consideration of his dreams.

Those who knew him not only as a psychologist, lecturer, or writer, but as a friend, have experienced his immense gift for friendship. His marriage was the most beautiful expression of his unique and deep gift for relationship. To his colleagues, his death left a gap in analytical psychology difficult, indeed, to fill; to his friends, his death was an irredeemable loss.

But it would be wrong to close on this negative note. When he was told, in London in October 1960, of a medical diagnosis that left little hope, both he and his wife faced it with a courage and acceptance which was in itself the measure of the man and his spirit. All that mattered to him then was to concentrate on the essentials and to return to Israel, where he wanted to die. He consulted the Chinese *Book of Changes*, and received an answer that will be a comfort to all of us, giving, as it were, the essence of his life and achievement. It was Hexagram 14, Possession in Great Measure, with the judgment, "Supreme success." In the commentary to this hexagram we read: "Possession in great measure is determined by fate and accords with the time. . . . It is done by virtue of unselfish modesty. The time is favorable—a time of strength within, clarity and culture without. Power is expressing itself in a graceful and controlled way. This brings supreme success and wealth." And as if to make it clear that a final stage had been reached, there was no moving line.

Erich Neumann died at the height of his creative powers, and his death cut short many more projects in his mind. His posthumous—and sadly unfinished—monograph *The Child*, dealing with the "Structure and Dynamics of the Nascent Personality," first published in 1973, bears witness to his creativity, undiminished to the last.

His loss to analytical psychology is enormous. But

there is some comfort in the fact that the importance of his work is more widely recognized than ever and that the influence of his ideas is constantly growing. Of this the present edition of his essays bears significant witness. May this undertaking make his writings known to ever wider circles and help spread the enormous potentialities inherent in his thought.

Gerhard Adler

London, November 1960 / April 1978

CREATIVE MAN

The following essay originated as far back as 1933—i.e., a year before Neumann's first meeting with Jung, which was to have such a decisive impact on his later work. It is all the more remarkable that in this essay—really still the product of Neumann the philosopher, and not of Neumann the analytical psychologist—all the basic ideas of analytical psychology—for example, the complex, the archetype, the shadow, the anima, and the self—are either already included or else, as it were, can be glimpsed between the lines. The reader should bear in mind that Kafka was still a relatively unknown author in Germany at the time this essay was written and that very little of the great flood of publications about him which is available today existed at that period. Subsequently, as Erich Neumann's wife explained to me, her husband always hesitated to publish this essay in its original form; he intended to revise it and to bring it into line with the latest results of Kafka scholarship before he incorporated it into his collected works. His early death prevented the fulfillment of this project, so that the essay on Kafka remains a historical document from the early work of this distinguished analyst.

—Hans Dieckmann

I

KAFKA'S "THE TRIAL": AN INTERPRETATION THROUGH DEPTH PSYCHOLOGY

If a man does not judge himself, all things judge him,
and all things become the messengers of God.

Rabbi Nachman of Breslau

I

THE COURT

Joseph K. has been arrested. The whole thing is enigmatic. The prosecutor and the charge are unknown. It
is not even certain that a charge has been made. Proceedings have been instituted: that is all. By a person
unknown versus Joseph K. Nobody knows what has

"Franz Kafka: Das Gericht; Eine tiefenpsychologische Deutung,"
Analytische Psychologie (Berlin), v:4 (1974). The forenote is
extracted from foreword to the same publication. For other
details, see the editorial note to the present volume.

Quotations from *The Trial* are based on the translation of
Edwin and Willa Muir (New York: Knopf; and London: Secker
and Warburg, 1937; revised by E. M. Butler, 1956).

happened. The warders who have been sent out and the Inspector who duly informs K. of the arrest are none of them responsible. They act and carry out instructions, but have no idea why this should have happened to K. The way K. accepts the arrest is as enigmatic as the arrest itself. The surprising thing is that he gives in. He holds up his coat "as if displaying it to the warders for their approval"—it is as if he has "in a way admitted the strangers' right to an interest in his actions." After suddenly becoming the center of a completely unintelligible happening, which was in flat contradiction of all normal reality, he says, "Certainly, I am surprised, but I am not by any means very surprised."

He protests, he is ironical, he regards the whole thing as a joke, he is quite sure it must be a mistake; yet more astonishing than anything that happens is the way in which Joseph K. recognizes and accepts the trial, and even to some extent realizes what he is doing. He does not want to dress, yet he does so, he wants to call an advocate, yet he does not do so, he protests against everything—and then gives in.

He is always concerned to retain his superiority, yet underneath he is permeated by a growing fear. But that is not true! *He* is not afraid. He, Joseph K., is convinced that you have only to clear away the disorder in the household and "every trace of these events would be obliterated and things would resume their usual course." And yet secretly something in him *is* afraid, something is in a state of such panic fear that when the warders leave him alone, he is surprised, because he "had abundant opportunities to take his life."

Admittedly, K. never loses control. He always knows

immediately when his thoughts are absurd; he also knows, in relation to Frau Grubach, how he really ought to have behaved, and what really ought to have been done; he is very conscious and superior—yet at the same time he is surprised that the events of that morning should have made him consider giving notice to Frau Grubach, and he is frightened by the house-porter's son in the street doorway. What shows him up more than anything, though, is the sympathy shown him by Frau Grubach and the tears in her voice as she begs him, "Don't take it so much to heart, Herr K."

Yet the strangest thing of all is not K.'s unconscious fear, but his feeling of guilt, which breaks through over and over again. It is true that K. says—and we have no reason to doubt his sincerity here—that he "cannot recall the slightest offense that might be charged against him"; yet unexpectedly, out of some deep level inaccessible to his conscious awareness, the cry breaks out in his conversation with Frau Grubach, "If you want to keep your house respectable you'll have to begin by giving me notice!" And then in a flash the thought struck him, "Will she take my hand?"

The relationship with Fräulein Bürstner, too, which is initiated so abruptly that it is almost like an assault, is really an attempt to escape and an appeal for help and protection. The scene of his arrest, which he has just said he regards as "a pure figment," in fact haunts him to such an extent and is so "horrible" that he feels obliged to repeat it as though he were under a compulsion. He broods more and more over the warders' statement that there can be no question of the Court's making a mistake; yet we are also told that "before going to sleep he thought for a little while about his behavior; he was pleased with it, yet surprised that he was not still more pleased."

Again and again we meet with the same kind of division. We never hear of K. taking steps of any kind to throw light on the nature of the events which have overtaken him. We are told, it is true, that "he was always inclined to take things easily, to believe in the worst only when the worst happened, to take no care for the morrow even when the outlook was threatening"; yet his complete indifference about the nature of his arrest, the lack of interest, which permits of no attempt to gather information or to make enquiries, is conspicuous. Corresponding to this impassivity but in a more active mode is the matter-of-fact way in which K. sets out to keep his appointment with the Examining Magistrate. He mobilizes all the usual protests and cynical defenses—but he goes. Just on the decisive issue, he accepts. Everything else is an arabesque around the basic fact of his obedience, while at the same time K. himself remains unconscious of this basic fact and his conscious attitude is still obsessively negative.

Externally, this division reveals itself in the way in which K. "knows" the time of his appointment, although he has not been directly informed about it. He "wants" to arrive late, without noticing that this intention clearly implies an exact knowledge of the time when he is in fact expected. He does not notice that his faulty intention corresponds to an enigmatic knowledge of the appointed time. Typical of K. is the feeling of innocence to which he clings; he is convinced that he has not been told when he ought to come. His "knowledge" is not real; how can he know when he has not been told? K. does not suspect for a moment that this "unreal" knowledge actually determines, although negatively, his intention to arrive late. Here the split psychology produces a grotesque compromise: K. finally *runs* in order to arrive "on time"! In this act of running, his knowledge of the right time has broken through once again; he obeys neither his knowledge nor his counterintention to disobey it.

The curious way in which K. finds the Interrogation Commission provides us with another enigma. As he wishes "to get a chance of looking into the rooms," he enquires after a nonexistent "joiner called Lanz." He rejects the idea of asking for the room occupied by the Interrogation Commission because that might injure his reputation. The result is a long and pointless expedition through the house. The plan which at first seemed so practical declares its independence of his purpose. "In this way" K. was finally "conducted over the whole floor." He already intends to go home, but turns back again, for the first time with real resolution, and the watchword "a joiner called Lanz," with which he now knocks on the door of the first room, leads him, surprisingly and inexplicably, to the Interrogation Commission. He is not told that a joiner called Lanz really lives there, yet in answer to his question he is immediately shown the right way. It is as if his intention, which is now genuine, to find the Interrogation Commission has made the watchword "a joiner called Lanz" transparent, so that, in spite of this question and in fact directly *through* it, his meaning is understood and he is shown the way he is trying to find.

On his arrival, K. is informed that he is an hour and

five minutes late; and it turns out that the appointment has in fact been fixed at the time which was "known" to K. The way in which K. finds the Interrogation Commission as soon as he really looks for it, and the agreement between the time fixed by the Court and his own inner knowledge actually belong to the same context. In the first place, we have the remarkable phenomenon of the "adaptability of the trial." The trial seems to fit in with K. When he is not really looking for the room and his reputation is more important to him than finding it, the room is not to be discovered, though K. wanders right through the house; yet the moment he starts looking in earnest, he finds the Commission behind the first door. On the other hand, though no appointed time has been given K., it turns out that the time he himself has fixed as "correct," the time which he "knew," is in fact "valid" for the authorities. It is quite clear that if K. had fixed a later hour, that too would have been valid for the Court.

At first sight this may sound improbable, but in fact it is the only conceivable way in which it is possible for us to explain how K. succeeded in locating the Commission at all by the use of such a watchword as "a joiner called Lanz." In itself, the verbal formula is completely irrelevant: it is simply a symbol for K.'s intention "to find or not to find" as the case may be. The only reality here is his own inner attitude; this is what shines through the transparency of the watchword. The adaptability of the Trial means precisely that it turns up wherever K. is looking for it and is not to be found wherever he does not look for it. And vice versa, this same adaptability implies that the Trial is always to be found where K.

8

inwardly "places" it, "knows" it to be, "looks for" it, and "wills" it to be. The procedure of the Trial fits in with the accused. The location of the room is just as much determined by K. as the time of the interrogation. K. even suspects this when he plays with the notion that if the Court is attracted by the guilt of the accused, the Interrogation Commission ought really to be located on the particular flight of stairs which he himself happens to choose. This knowledge of K.'s is also derived from that layer of his mind which in some quite unspecified sense knows him to be guilty. As long as he obeys the dictates of his reputation, his ego-consciousness, this knowledge possesses no validity and is in fact false—and so he wanders through the house. But when he really looks for the Interrogation Commission, he is obeying the deep layer in himself and knows that he is accused and that he is guilty; and then the correctness of his knowledge is at once confirmed and the Commission is behind the first door that he happens to choose.

The delay involved in K.'s arriving too late corresponds to his failure to take the Trial seriously. If K. had arrived at what he "knew" was the right time, and if he had at once really tried to find the Interrogation Commission, the Interrogation Chamber would certainly have been located on the particular flight which K. had happened to choose, behind the first door which he had happened to open. The phenomenon of the "adaptability of the Trial" also provides us with evidence that the Court "overlaps" the ordinary workaday world of outer reality; it does not collide with it, but is in a strange way "resident in its midst." In spite of all its concreteness the

Trial does have an air of "unreality" about it, in the sense, that is, that there is a marked discrepancy between it and "ordinary" reality. No doubt that is what Frau Grubach meant when she said, "This arrest . . . gives me the feeling of something very learned."

The intermediate sphere in which the Trial takes place is determined by the behavior of the accused; yet the Court again carries the day against the accused precisely because the accused "gives in." The adaptability of the Trial and the reality of K.'s inner knowledge are interdependent. K. has an inkling of this as he implies when he tells the Interrogation Commission later on, "It is only a Trial if I recognize it as such." As we have just seen, the Trial is "there" when K. recognizes it, and is not there when he only pretends to look for it, i.e., when he does not take it seriously or recognize it.

Here we encounter an extremely significant relationship of interdependence between the arrested man and the prosecuting authority, which will occupy us at length later on. Yet no less striking, in the same context, is the split in K.'s own psychology, which is responsible for his half-conscious, half-unconscious recognition of the Trial, and also for a diametrically opposite attitude. This opposite attitude, which regards the whole thing as an incredible and improbable joke, is the ruling constellation that dominates K.'s ego-consciousness, and is shown quite clearly by his behavior before the Investigating Commission.

He completely fails to recognize his real situation, appears in the guise of a reformer, an accuser and even a chairman, and finally strikes the table with his fist and declares, "I beg you to postpone until later any comments you may wish to exchange on what I have to say, for I am pressed for time and must leave very soon." He tries to intervene when the washerwoman is embraced by a man at the back of the hall, and it is not until the end, when he is detained by force, that he recognizes that the forum before which he has spoken does in fact belong to the Court. It is only the badges worn by the officials which finally convince him that he has not been addressing a party meeting, with friends and enemies, an audience and a public, but that he has in fact been standing before a great Investigation Commission.

K.'s speech is a matchless example of public abuse, powered by an affect which contrasts in the most astonishing way with his normal indifference to the Trial. All his doubts and uncertainties, secret fears and feelings of guilt are unloaded in an outburst which is in equal measure brutal, reckless, and panic-stricken. "Keep off or I'll strike you," cried K. to a trembling old man who had pushed quite close to him. No one would have imagined that the "junior manager of a large bank" who is a stickler for good form would be capable of such conduct. "Scoundrels" and "corrupt band"—such are the expressions used by a man who is so sensitive that he will be disturbed by a colleague's smile at the office. This violent emotion is all the more remarkable if we remember that no one compelled K. to go to the Investigation Commission and that he has in fact taken great pains to find it. After he himself has said that the Trial stands or falls with his recognition of it, he does emphatically recognize it "for the moment" and in so doing places himself within the jurisdiction of the Court. And then he behaves in this senseless manner! But assuming that the task of the Investigation Commission is to examine K. and to find out "who" he is, then we must admit that the Commission succeeds in enticing the accused man out of his fortress with uncanny and unholy speed. And if we adopt the standpoint of the judges, which is that "the high authorities—before they would order such an arrest as this—must be quite well informed about the reasons for the arrest and the person of the prisoner," then precisely in this context the Examining Magistrate's strange question, "Well, then, you are a house-painter?" appears in a new and peculiar light. This apparently harmless and nonsensical question in fact provokes K.'s outburst, the speech in which he so fatally exposes himself. In order to realize how far this question actually takes the Examining Magistrate—whether or not it was a deliberately selected stimulus question or an "accident"—we have only to picture what a different person K. would have had to be if he had given a quick and objective answer. It is significant that there is a passage in *The Castle* which informs us that accidents are always on the side of the authorities.

It would be a mistake to read into this question some malicious intent, quite apart from the fact that in his capacity as an official the Examining Magistrate is obviously doing his duty—which is to examine! On the contrary, the Trial is characterized from the outset by a remarkable spirit of friendliness. The warders and the Inspector are not only forthcoming beyond the requirements of their official duties, but the advice, information, and guidance which they offer would have been extremely helpful to K. if he had considered them worthy of his attention. The way in which the time for the appointment is arranged and the willingness of the Examining Magistrate to interrogate K. in spite of his lateness are evidence of an unusual degree of consideration for him. All this is summarized in the principle laid down by the Inspector at the time of the arrest: "You won't be hampered in carrying on in the ordinary course of your life."

Yet that is not the whole story. All the people with whom K. comes into contact are particularly friendly towards him—Frau Grubach and Fräulein Bürstner, the Manager and the Deputy Manager, and the people in the house who help him to look for the joiner called Lanz. Everyone in fact is ready to help him, the "world" is not hostile, but kind and helpful, although—as is clear from the case of the joiner called Lanz—they are not in a position to give him real help. Without knowing it, these people in the house are dominated by K.'s will to arrive late; they are unsuspecting tools of his faulty attitude. For them, the joiner Lanz is a human being whom he is looking for and whom they are helping him to find, not a symbol behind which his will to find the Court or not to find the Court is the effective agent. They are simply concretizations of his negative will, and their helpfulness towards him is not and cannot be really effective. In spite of all their helpfulness he is living, as it were, in empty space, since the question at issue is his recognition or nonrecognition of the Trial, and this is a conflict which cannot be touched by the helpful attempts of these people to find a "real" "joiner Lanz."

But just as the innocence of helpful people—in a way that is uncanny and by no means innocent—subserves the purpose of K.'s will to procrastinate without his becoming aware of the fact, so too when he stands before the Interrogation Commission he sees nothing but "members of the public" in the uniformed officials who in fact belong to the Court. He never senses what lies behind things, he is never in touch with what is "really" going on, and it is precisely this that confuses him so much and leads him astray the whole time. He himself lives in an innocent relationship with his ego-consciousness, which is in stark contrast to the deeper knowledge possessed by the other side of his nature. He really knows that whether or not he finds the room depends upon himself and not upon strange people hunting around for a nonexistent "joiner called Lanz"; and he also knows that an appearance before an Investigation Commission is a challenge which requires caution and presence of mind.

K.'s behavior before the Investigation Commission would be understandable if it were really true that the Trial had not yet made the slightest emotional impact upon him. In fact, however, his train of thought while he was looking for the Commission and his remark about the necessity for a recognition of the Trial by himself contradicts that. And his comment later on about the "great organization" which exists behind everything is equally striking. Even though his negative attitude, with its aggressiveness and protest, usurps the foreground, and now as always, the great organization is only an object of abuse, the point we have to bear in mind in this context is that K. is not "ignorant." Part of him knows perfectly well what is going on and what lies hidden behind the façade—for example behind the particular official who is confronting him at the moment. And this part of K.'s nature is equally well-informed about the legitimacy of what is happening. K.'s conscious behavior must obviously be viewed in a more serious light for this reason, since he makes absolutely no use of his other "knowledge" and in fact carries on as if it did not exist. In this sense, too, K. is not "innocent." In any case, as the Examining Magistrate put it, K. has "flung away with his own hand all the advantages which an interrogation invariably confers on an accused man." The Trial has now entered on a new stage. It will undoubtedly continue— that has been certain from the outset, but owing to K.'s behavior it has taken on an even more uncanny atmosphere than before. In future, there will be no recurrence of the kind of clear-cut situation in which K. appears before an Interrogation Commission. Prescisely when he is not thinking about it and is in fact entirely unprepared, the Interrogation Commission will be able to observe him, which means that he has also flung away the protection which is always afforded by a knowledge that the crucial moment is precisely the present. Characteristically, K.'s first attempt to make a real contact with the Court involves a relationship with a woman. K. makes up his mind to triumph over the Court by enticing the wife of the Law Court Attendant away from a student of the Law. This attempt is not only pointless and ridiculous;

it is a total failure. The woman betrays him and leaves him in the lurch. K. is not even startled for a moment. He completely fails to understand that however strange her way of showing it may be, this woman, by giving herself to the student, is really devoting herself to the great organization and that her aim is actually to serve it. K. does not even gain an insight into the power structure of the Court as a result of this incident. The Law Court Attendant indicates to K. that even the student is extremely influential and that K. can only risk everything because he is in any case lost, since "none of our cases can be regarded as capable of failing." K. takes no notice of this. Neither his own experiences nor the information he has received about the thoroughness of the proceedings and the tireless industry and serious-mindedness of the Examining Magistrates make the slightest impression on him. He remains foolish and cynical and exposes his egotism only too obviously when he, the supposed reformer, without hesitation declares that "he wouldn't have lost an hour's sleep over the need for reforming the machinery of justice" in the Court if it hadn't been a matter of life and death to himself.

As he makes his way into the Law Court offices the situation of the accused is demonstrated to him in the most cruel terms, but K. relates none of this to his own case. In the Law Court offices K. is for the first time fully exposed to the atmosphere of the Court. For a while he passes through the ranks of the accused unsuspectingly, as a stranger, and is only disconcerted by the incomprehensibility and pointlessness of their behavior, but very soon he too is caught up in it.

The girl in the Law Court offices whose face has "that severe look which the faces of many women have in the first flower of their youth" and the man who "has an answer to every question," the Clerk of Inquiries, come to meet him, without K. having taken any initiative. They are living witnesses to the truth of what the girl herself is concerned to explain to him—i.e., that the Law Court officials are not hard-hearted. They help him, they actually invite him to consult the Clerk of Inquiries, but the effect on K. is exactly as if not a word of all this had been spoken. Never throughout the course of the Trial does he remember either the Clerk of Inquiries or the tenderness and kindness of the girl, who is an official of the Court. The admonition of the Clerk of Inquiries, who told an overzealous accused man, with an unmistakable reference to K., "When one sees so many people who scandalously neglect their duty, one learns to have patience with men like you," goes over K.'s head without producing the slightest impact.

For a moment, it is true, it does occur to K. to wonder whether he ought to enquire about the next interrogation, and for a moment it does look as if he means to revise radically his attitude to the Interrogation Commission and the Court—and for a moment the girl, the Law Court Attendant and the Clerk of Inquiries (who is now approaching) look at him hopefully, "as if they expected some immense transformation to happen to him the next moment, a transformation which they did not want to miss"—but it was only a physical feeling of malaise. As the Clerk of Inquiries ironically remarks, "It's only here that this gentleman feels unwell, not in other places."

The atmosphere of the Court produces a kind of disturbance of balance, a feeling of dizziness, but in K.'s case the shift in balance is by no means in the direction of the "knowing" part of his nature. His ego-consciousness is almost paralyzed, but all that "is" nothing and means nothing.

K. can scarcely shut the door quickly enough which separates the normal world from the world of the Law Court offices and the Court. It was nothing but a physical feeling of faintness: in a way that is typical and characteristic of all K.'s, everything is sidetracked and projected onto something that is "real" and uncompromisingly external. No insight, no reflection, no fruitful doubt remains. The sole result of K.'s first visit to the world of the Court is a misgiving about the integrity of his physical health, and the notion that he should consult a doctor at the earliest opportunity.

So it seems. And yet when he wonders, "Could his *body* possibly be meditating a revolution and preparing to spring a new Trial on him, since he had borne with the old one so effortlessly?" something far more uncanny is looming behind this reflection. His uncertainty is really the outcome of an obscure intuition, which senses how deeply the split has already penetrated within him. His mistrust of his own body, the most real and actual part of a man, is only a symbol that shows how keenly K. feels the real ground of his existence, his very foundation, quaking beneath him. This strangeness and mistrust in relation to his body is proof positive of the split and alienation which divide K.'s ego-consciousness from the "knowing" foundation of his nature. It is proof positive that the Court has "arrested" his body, his foundation, and that the Trial is advancing within K. and is steadily gaining ground in his own country.

In spite of this, however, K. is not entirely wrong in his charge against the authorities. Is it not a fact that he has denounced genuine abuses? For example, is it really possible to defend the conduct of the warders at the time of K.'s arrest, when they ate up his breakfast and made no secret of their intention to enrich themselves by annexing his personal belongings?

In the chapter entitled "The Whipper," this question is given a very strange answer, which introduces us at the deepest level into the inner situation of Herr K. and into a discussion of the whole problem of guilt and justice.

When K. opens the storeroom door at the office, he does not suspect that the Trial has extended its sphere of activity and has forced its way into the office where he works. He has not the slightest idea what is going on, and it is only the complaints of the warders and the information supplied by the Whipper that acquaint him with the actual state of affairs. The warders are being whipped because K. has, justifiably, complained about them to the Examining Magistrate. K., however, takes no interest in what is happening, it does not seem to concern him in the least, he does not notice that the Court, which is supposedly so negligent, has taken immediate steps to punish the warders, nor does he realize that he is the cause of this whipping. We are no longer surprised when the warders' remark about the disaster of being an accused man does not cause K. any anxiety.

However, K.'s attempt to buy the release of the

warders is certainly curious. Among other charges that he has cast in the teeth of the administration of the Court is precisely corruption—but of course *his* attempt at corruption is part of his battle against the corrupt administration of the Court. Though he himself has informed against the warders and demanded their punishment and the warders themselves have actually admitted their guilt, K. suddenly argues that the warders are not to blame, but that "it was the organization, it was the high officials who were to blame."

Yet what is the truth about the great organization, what is its attitude towards its subordinate functionaries, towards the warders and the Whipper?

Already at the time of the original arrest the warders had displayed some remarkable qualities. They had combined an awareness of their subordinate status with an absolutely firm grasp of the infallibility of the high authorities and of the inadequacy of K.'s line of argument. They not only showed themselves excellently informed about the Law and the nature of the Court, they also tried to help K., to instruct him and to enlighten him about the attitude that he ought to adopt towards the Trial and towards himself. Their negative private behavior, the way they scrounged K.'s breakfast and tried to walk off with his clothes, is of entirely secondary importance. This was a "trespass" on the negative side just as their friendly behavior was a trespass on the positive side, and it is by no means impossible that the habitual toleration of these abuses by the organization actually takes this into account. It is true that such conduct is forbidden by the authorities, yet the point of view ex-

pressed by the warders when they ask, "What importance
can such things have for a man who is unlucky enough
to be arrested?" may also, though not openly admitted,
hold good of the authorities, for whom such things are
"insignificant." In spite of this, however, the warders
have to be punished if K. complains about them. Their
punishment, as the Whipper says, is "as just as it is inevitable."

Strictly speaking, toleration of the private freedom of
its executive functionaries by the great organization is a
concession to the accused. Trespasses of this kind make
it far easier for him to orientate himself. Yet every trespass, every deviation from the prescribed path of duty
in the procedure of the Trial represents a risk for the
trespasser. If the accused rejects the trespass and thrusts
the officials back, as it were, within the limits of the Law
and of the exact mechanism of the Trial, then he must
be obeyed, since for this purpose he is the highest authority in the Trial. The accused is entitled to insist on
his formal right that the officials shall in fact do their
duty, even when the trespass has been committed out of
feelings of friendship towards him, but particularly of
course when these friendly feelings have resulted in some
form of material reward. Equally obvious, however, is
the consequence of K.'s behavior. The Whipper actually
draws this consequence when in answer to K.'s attempt
at bribery he says, "So you want to lay a complaint
against me too and get me a whipping as well? No, No!"
And then, "What you say sounds reasonable enough, but
I refuse to be bribed. I am here to whip people, and whip
them I shall." That is the clear, cold performance of

duty, without transgression and without any form of partial private freedom. In Kant's language it is "the official an sich," the official "in himself," so that it represents what K. had really demanded. And at this stage it suddenly becomes clear that if the Trial were in fact as K. had demanded, it would be cruel and inexorable beyond all hope, a machine without joints that would crush the accused and deny him the slightest chance of escaping, of prolonging the Trial, or even of living.

That K. should fail to fathom the real state of affairs is not perhaps surprising; what is astonishing is his failure to grasp the connection between his complaint and the Whipper; he simply does not want to know about it. When he evades this problem and maintains that it was not the warders who were to blame, but the organization and the high officials, he is right, though without having right on his side. That is what is so strange and confusing. K. often says something that is correct without correctly grasping its full significance; he "knows" about basic and crucial realities, yet at the same time he interprets them wrongly.

The high authorities have in principle permitted the partial private freedom of their executive functionaries and are therefore in fact partly responsible for their misbehavior. K. is intelligent enough to realize this, yet consistently he only sees the negative side of everything, so that, for example, he completely fails to recognize this is really a concession, a friendly action, towards himself.

Our mention of this characteristic of K.'s does perhaps bring us closer to his own real guilt and the circumstances that resulted in his indictment, or rather arrest. What the father said to his son Georg in *The Judgment* could equally well be applied to Joseph K. "You were really an innocent child, but more really still, a devilish human being."

It is already quite clear that K. is irresponsible, arrogant, vain and, in relation to himself, untruthful; yet all these negative qualities might also, in a certain sense, be no more than childishly unconscious. There are, however, numerous facts that throw a very different light on K.'s character. His inability to appreciate friendliness and helpfulness in others directs our attention to his relationship to people in general; and at this point something very striking does emerge. His deliberately brusque and intimidating behavior towards Frau Grubach, the way in which he proposes to take advantage of Fräulein Bürstner, while completely disregarding her existence as a human being ("he knew that Fräulein B. was an ordinary little typist who would not resist him for long"), his negligent attitude towards his clerks' fate ("one of whom I shall dismiss at the earliest opportunity"), his relationship with the wife of the Law Court Attendant, of whom he also proposes to take advantage (he finds her "not altogether worthless" and thinks, "Probably there could be no more fitting revenge on the Examining Magistrate and his adherents than to wrest this woman from them and take her himself")—it is the same story all along. K.'s bright idea of involving the Law student in a liaison with Elsa and his pleasure at the thought of the situation that would arise "if this wretched student, this puffed-up child, this bandylegged twiddle-beard, had to kneel by Elsa's bed wringing his hands and begging for favors" is another instance. In fact, it is possible to multiply examples of qualities which prove how "bad" K. really is, how callous, brutal, narrow-minded, and egoistic. He never thinks of other people, but always and exclusively of himself. His inability to appreciate kindness and humanity in other people, his own hard-heartedness and coldness, and his inability to learn anything or to relate anything to himself are closely interdependent characteristics.

Although K. is "more really still a devilish human being," he is not a villain or an exceptional human being or even an exceptionally bad human being. What matters is that he is a human being like other human beings. He is like us all, and no one is entitled to wax indignant at his expense. The basic fact that Joseph K. is "one of us" is nowhere stated by Kafka; it is, however, an essential feature of his method of presenting his story. Every reader identifies himself with K.; he is compelled to do so for the time being. Everyone feels "injustice" whenever K. feels it and exclaims "Infernal nonsense!" whenever he does. With K., everyone feels sick in the dust of the Law Court offices and, with K., is only too glad to slam the door that keeps this embarrassing intermediate world at a distance. This too is the source of the endless misunderstandings which were revealed by the differing interpretations of the Trial. Owing to his identification with K., the reader experiences the events of the Trial in his own person; that is, in fact, the precise meaning of this "novel," for the basic situation of Joseph K., as a result of which he is arrested, is our own.

K. is never simply bad, he is always "a mixture." He desires the wife of the Law Court Attendant—and plans to obtain something by means of her. He seeks maternal comfort and aid from Fräulein Bürstner—and plans to take advantage of her. K. does nothing which is unexpected or out of the ordinary; in fact you might almost say that his behavior is "natural" and in a certain sense innocently childish, whereas what is required of him is something "learned," as Frau Grubach said.

On the other hand, it is clearly indicated, and is in fact constantly being urged upon K., that he should not behave as he actually does. Yet the tremendous stubbornness of his nature and of human nature in general—this slothfulness of the heart in the most threatening sense of the term—impedes all change or insight. A single sentence from the Trial might serve as a headline for K.'s entire life: "Before he fell asleep he thought for a little about his behavior, he was pleased with it, yet surprised that he was not still more pleased."

This problem comes to a head in the Whipper chapter, immediately after K.'s attempt to avert the punishment of the warders by bribery.

When the Whipper makes a cut at the warder Franz, "Then the shriek arose from Franz's throat, single and irrevocable, it did not seem to come from a human being but from some tortured instrument, the whole corridor rang with it, the whole building must hear it. 'Don't yell,' cried K., he was beside himself, he stood staring in the direction from which the clerks must presently come running, but he gave Franz a push, not a violent one but violent enough to make the half-senseless man fall and convulsively claw at the floor with his hands."

After K. has slammed the door of the whipping chamber, the clerks come along, ask him what he wants, and go away again. And then K. falls into a dreamily oppressive state, a tired twilight mood. He is looking down into a dark courtyard, and a strange interior discussion takes place in his mind.

He is assailed by torment, a torment of guilt because he has not been able to prevent the whipping. Immediately he tries to tear out the evil thing by the roots. It is not his fault, Franz's shriek has destroyed everything. We may ask ourselves, and K. does in effect ask himself, how this shriek is supposed to have made the annulment of the penalty impossible when it is actually only an expression of the torture caused by the penalty. But "K. could not afford to let the attendants and possibly all sorts of other people arrive and surprise him in a scene with these creatures in the storeroom."

What we have here is not just one of K.'s many egoistical character traits; something more had happened on this occasion. Wherever the Intermediate World appears, the Trial appears—and that may involve examination. K. did not intervene, he did not prevent the execution of the penalty—whether it could, objectively, have been averted is beside the question—and he failed to do so for the crassest egoistical reasons, quite blatantly to preserve his own reputation. His whole reasoning, his whole line of argument for the liberation of the warders, is suddenly unmasked; all at once he is guilty of the punishment of the warders in an entirely new sense, which has nothing to do with the fact that as a complainant before the Interrogation Commission he had actually brought about the punishment of the warders.

Once again, we observe the uncanny and illuminating ambiguity of the situation. If, as the Whipper said, the punishment is "just and inevitable," then the authorities are really in the ultimate analysis responsible, K.'s complaint works itself out within this whole system, and K. is really not "guilty" of the judgment. The action takes place exclusively in the legal sphere and the penalty cannot be charged to K.'s account. Since, however, the Whipper—in K.'s eyes, at any rate—also possesses a partial private freedom and is open to influence by K., even if only in the form of bribery, it follows that K. too is free within this system, in the sense that the penalty has been made dependent upon his conduct. And now, as if this situation was also somehow "intended" by the authorities, something happens that radically alters K.'s position. Franz's shriek deprives K. of the power to help the warders simply by using his checkbook. He is confronted by the consequences of his own intervention.

If he intervenes, he has to be prepared to risk his reputation. The liberation of the warders demands a genuine act of human commitment. Faced with this situation, K. repudiates the warder and slams the door. He has completely failed the test.

This incident makes it clear that it is possible to incur an obligation—e.g., a duty to intervene—even in a situation which in point of fact is beyond the scope of human intervention and interference. The illusion of free will is sufficient to create a valid moral responsibility.

So it is the consciousness of his own moral failure that is the real subject of his inner discussion; and its starting point is a feeling of torment.

K. takes the view that the sacrifice which the situation demanded should not really have been required of him. Yet there is something inside him that seems to desire nothing less than this sacrifice, and K.'s whole debate within himself has no other purpose than to silence this inner voice.

"If a sacrifice had been needed, it would almost have been simpler to take off his own clothes and offer himself as a substitute for the warders."

It is extremely startling to see this thought suddenly emerging in K.'s conscious mind. Although the argument that the Whipper would not have accepted him as a substitute serves the purpose of repressing this thought once again, we cannot help noticing how instinctively K. is already thinking "in terms of the system" and how profoundly he has really entered into the strictness and justice of the proceedings, which guarantee the immunity of the accused in relation to all the functionaries of the Court. It is this immunity that makes K.'s behavior possible in the first place, though it also entices him to expose himself, since there is no resistance against which he can regulate his conduct. It would almost appear as if this notion of sacrifice which springs up so quickly and is at once rejected might represent a crucial turning point in the proceedings. K.'s strange objection, "though of

course ordinary standards might not apply here either"
supports this conjecture. Perhaps a way of escape from
the Trial might have been found in this direction. If K.
had offered himself to the Whipper as a substitute, would
he not, by taking over the punishment in this way, have
raised himself above the level of the proceedings of the
Trial? Would he not by this action have transcended his
status as an accused man and by this resolution have
created an entirely new basis for his life?

Here again the point should be made that such an action, though astonishing, would have been in a sense altogether possible; it was by no means simply out of the
question. The thought comes entirely from K.'s own
mind; it occupies his attention and he discusses it with
himself for quite a long time.

In the Law Court offices the girl and the official had
gazed expectantly at K. as if something surprising might
suddenly happen, and it almost seems as if at that moment they were waiting for something which usually
plays a great part in all trials, but which in this case is
never mentioned and appears never to have been considered at all—i.e., a confession.

The sacrifice that would have been involved if K. had
offered himself as a substitute for the warders would
have been more than a simple confession, but a confession would have been necessary as the basis of this act,
and this would have been a confession of guilt, even if
only of guilt for the punishment of the warders.

At the end of this inner discussion, K.'s moral failure
is repeated. He says, "Even that action had not shut off
all danger," and realizes, "It was a pity that he had given

Franz a push at the last moment." As always, K. has "dealt with" every aspect. "They were past help by this time, and the clerks might appear at any moment; but he made a vow not to hush up the incident and to deal trenchantly, so far as lay in his power, with the real culprits, the higher officials."

Previously, though rich in inner happenings, the Trial has always been self-contained; it has never broken out of the prescribed framework. The bizarre events of the Whipper scene find their parallel in other scenes which are no less extraordinary. But K.'s uneasiness on the following day shows quite clearly that he has not recovered from it, and that his experience with the warders preoccupies him more than the other events of the Trial. And then something uncanny happens, something monstrous and horrifying. As he passed the storeroom, "he could not resist opening the door. And what confronted him, instead of the darkness he had expected, bewildered him completely. Everything was still the same, exactly as he had found it on opening the door the previous evening. . . . The Whipper with his rod and the warders with all their clothes on were still standing there, the candle was burning on the shelf, and the warders immediately began to cry out: 'Sir!' At once K. slammed the door shut and then beat on it with his fists, as if that would shut it more securely. He ran almost weeping to the clerks. . . . 'Clear that storeroom out, can't you?' he shouted. 'We're being smothered in dirt!'" And then we are told, "He sat down for a few moments, for the sake of their company," and later, "went home, tired, his mind quite blank."

We have quoted this passage at length because it is instructive in every respect. It is a remarkable continuation of the inner discussion of the previous day. If any kind of doubt still remained as to whether K. had failed in his duty in this situation, that doubt is no longer tenable now. If K. had been surprised by the suddenness of Franz's shriek and had only slammed the door in his initial alarm, then a very generous, very kind Court might not find it necessary to count this particular "examination situation" against him and might order the examination to be repeated.

Perhaps it was not intended that the opportunity implicit in K.'s idea of sacrifice should be allowed to go by without use being made of it; if the same situation was offered to him once again and he was given time to think it over, perhaps he would seize the opportunity.

But if this repetition of the event is to bear the meaning we have suggested, how can such a practice possibly be reconciled with the basic presuppositions of the Trial? Is not this kind of repeat performance, especially staged, as it were, for K., in flat contradiction to the whole ethos of the Court? And what would become of the "objective side" of the Whipper scene? After all, the warders are not simply "philosophical fictions."

We can only answer these questions if we bear in mind the extraordinary ambiguity and equivocalness of these happenings, which are still, however, in our view by no means beyond the range of our understanding. There is no evidence that this repetition scene was "arranged" for K. It is by no means impossible that the punishment of the warders by the Whipper has to be carried out on several different days, but that in spite of this the relationship between K. and the warders is also taken into account by the authorities. Justice would require that the warders should also be given the benefit of the chance that K. might ransom them by his self-offering, just as they had only been sentenced to their punishment as a result of his accusation in the first place. This means that the situation K. finds himself confronted with may be entirely "objective" in the sense that it is independent of K.'s subjective conception of the circumstances. Moreover, although, as on the first occasion, the situation may be, in subjective terms, beyond the range of K.'s power to exert any influence, the attitude he adopts towards it may still be the decisive factor on which the future course of the Trial will depend. We have seen how K. may be ethically responsible for an event whose occurrence is in itself necessary (and therefore in point of fact beyond the scope of his free will); in the same way an event can, in relation to K., be there "for him," although its occurrence is in itself necessary and it would happen even if K. was not required to take up an attitude towards it.

There is, however, one further aspect which demands our attention and which at first sight seems to be at variance with everything else. How are we to understand the extraordinary part that is played by "the door"? This was already a decisive factor when K. first visited the Law Court offices, and then as now the world that it cuts off from K. is very curiously located in the normal world. Then it was situated in the attics at the top of a tenement building; now it is in a storeroom. On both

occasions the world of the Court that had been established there had become "unreal" and submerged at the
slamming of the door. That the atmosphere "behind the
door" differs in principle from the air of the real, physical world requires no further demonstrations; however,
the transformation that takes place when the door is
slammed is of the greatest significance. In the first case,
after K.'s visit to the Law Court offices we are told, "And
then (K.) leaped down the stairs so buoyantly and with
such long strides that he became almost afraid of his
own reaction." This time we read, "The shrieks had
completely stopped." What happens in both these cases
is that the scene disappears into an "interregnum"
which, although not unreal, is nevertheless real in a different sense from the everyday world. This world of the
Trial and of the Court, which is "resident in the midst
of the world of reality," stands in a specific relationship
to K., and in fact to all the accused. It is true that it always appears as quasi-real and is outwardly indistin-
guishable from the everyday world; in fact it actually
seems as if the clerks heard the shriek from the storeroom, although the text gives no explicit information on
this point. Yet the localization of this world, its atmosphere, and its extraordinary ability to appear anywhere
—in K.'s flat, in any house, in the attics, in the storeroom
—combine to give it an eerie quality.

We have already mentioned this quality of strangeness in another context, when we were considering the
problem of the "joiner called Lanz." We saw then that
the principle of the adaptation of the Trial and the way
in which it overlaps with reality corresponded with the

reality of K.'s inner knowledge and that what made this correspondence possible was the interdependence of the arrested man and the Trial situation.

It could be argued that what happened "behind the door" took place in K. himself, in a deeper region of his own personality, and that the "intermediate" reality of the Trial represented an inner reality of his own nature. In that case the slamming of the door would signify a violent turning away from this intermediate reality, which would also explain the half-real character of this world. It would be real within himself but unreal in the sense that when the door was slammed "the shrieks had completely stopped" and another person would have heard nothing.

It is true that many features of the novel can be understood along these lines, but in the case of very many others, including the most vital consideration of all, this approach in its simple form bars the way to any possibility of understanding.

The Trial, the proceedings, the officials, the entire happening in all its concreteness has a far wider significance than anything confined to K.'s personality. Kafka's uniformly concrete narrative and the accuracy of his diction preclude any simple reference back to K.'s own subjective psyche. In the Whipper scene, for example, we must clearly differentiate between the objective happenings and K.'s subjective situation and personal attitude towards them. The Trial is in fact actually constituted by the way in which K. defines his attitude to the real, objective proceedings of the Court, which are independent of his personality. On the other hand, the reliability of the text had also brought us back to the conclusion that we must be dealing with something intimately connected with K.'s own inner world. The problem of the "door" directed our attention to a crossing point between the objective and the subjective dimensions. We also found it essential not to forget that the "reality of the Court" was unmistakably different from "normal everyday reality."

And yet, wherever the intermediate reality appears, K. is invariably stimulated to participate in it, and he does this in an entirely personal way. He is profoundly involved in the sequence of events, even though it runs its course objectively and independently of himself. At the same time, however, the staff of the Court, including the warders and the Whipper in the storeroom, are, in spite of their objectivity, "real" in a different sense from Frau Grubach and Fräulein Bürstner, for example; they have a quite private relationship to K. and in fact belong to "his" Trial.

This can also be formulated in the following way. The Trial with its authorities, its officials and so on is something objective which exists before and after K., affects not only him but many others, and possesses institutions, organizations, servants and documents; yet in spite of all this, K. was right when he said, "It is only a trial if I recognize it as such."

We can now summarize our findings at this stage: (1) the intermediate world of the Trial is supposed to represent a transition between the subjective and the objective dimensions; (2) the Court, the authorities, etc. are an objective reality independent of K.'s personality,

CREATIVE MAN

but not interchangeable with the everyday reality of the outside world; (3) on the other hand, as we have pointed out several times, K. is the real stage on which the Trial takes place. It is, in a certain sense, a "trial within himself."

Kafka's narrative makes it necessary for us to assume that in addition to the subjective-psychic dimension in K. there exists an objective-psychic dimension that is just as "objective" (i.e., independent of K.) as the outside world and that is nevertheless at the same time "in" K. himself. K. "is" not this objective-psychic dimension any more than he "is" the outside world; he confronts it just as he confronts the outside world, and in fact he is not even fully conscious that this world is not outside himself. He experiences it as an "intermediate" reality, i.e., as distinguishable from the outside world and yet as a world outside. In relation to it he has the same "not-I" experience as he had in relation to the outside world.

But there is a part of K. that has a knowledge about this objective-psychic dimension, about its laws, and about the connection between the person K. and this world within himself. The split to which we have drawn attention so often arises simply because K., the "person" of the ego-consciousness, rejects the part of himself that knows and the whole objective-psychic world about which it knows and refuses to allow it to come into consciousness.

When this happens the objective-psychic world behaves exactly like an authority in the outside world which brings a lawsuit against a particular person. The

36

argument between the person K. and this world of the Court is "the Trial." With the aid of his split-off part K. "knows" about what is going on, about the organization and about the connection between the Trial and its recognition by himself. It is perfectly true that the objective-psychic dimension is a deep layer in K., but we must also realize that this "in K." does not refer to the personal psychic subjective realm in K. Precisely because this objective-psychic dimension is as much outside K.'s personal realm as the outside world is beyond K.'s ego-consciousness, we have decided to call it, by way of abbreviation, "the Trans." The Trans is a world, a hierarchical, ordered world, about whose "head" Kafka tells us nothing. It is in fact already implicit in this expression that only the lowest regions of this world are visible. The "high authorities" and "*the* Judge" are "beyond." In spite of this, the objective-psychic world of the Trans is not beyond experience; on the contrary, the Trial itself is nothing more nor less than the experience, the rejected experience, of the constitution of this objective-psychic dimension in the form of a Law and of a Court.

We have spoken about the split in K. and about a "knowing" part of him that we called his foundation; elsewhere we call this K.'s "transpersonal part" or simply his transpersonality. It is a part of K. which is beyond the personal realm; however, it should be understood that this personal realm includes the entire subjective-psychic dimension, i.e., not only ego-consciousness but also that part of the unconscious which is known as the personal unconscious. This transpersonality belongs to the objective-psychic dimension, to the Trans, in a sense which can only be made clear elsewhere, in another context.

The recognition of the Trial by K. becomes more and more obvious as the case proceeds; this interdependence between the accused man and the judicial institution of the Court is based on the fact that the part of K. which we have called his transpersonality also belongs to the Court:

It is this interdependence between K. as an accused man and the organization of the Court which makes possible the Court's intervention in the first place. We can now understand why the principle of the adaptation of the proceedings and the reality of their situation within the psyche actually refer to the same thing. They are two particular manifestations of the intermediate reality of the Trial. And we shall experience more and more vividly the inexorable advance of this process in which K. is appropriated by the Court. K.'s desperate and senseless defense against the Trial is in reality directed against his own inward psychological erosion. That is why his escape into extraversion is so essentially deluded; and that is why the Inspector told him, right at the beginning, at the time of his arrest, "Think less about us and what is going to happen to you, think more about yourself."

The slamming of the storeroom door, like that of the door to the Law Court offices, is really the slamming of an inner door; it represents K.'s turning away from the processes of the Trial, which takes place simultaneously within him and outside.

For K. the objective-psychic dimension appears "outside," in the form of an intermediate reality. This, however, is not simply Kafka's way of representing the situation—though the real objectivity and secularity of this psychic dimension cannot be represented in any other way—but it is one of the peculiarities of the Trans that it appears in a quasi-external manner. It is true that the injunction to "think more about yourself" does contain a hint that nothing short of genuine insight, looking within and becoming conscious, can make it possible to discern the true location of the Court; yet it is entirely normal and correct that the objective-psychic dimension should confront man as a "Trans," and that he should initially experience this inner Trans in projected form as a Trans outside.

What makes the world so uncanny for K. is precisely the fact that the "world" (i.e., that which is "outside") now consists of two dimensions, the normal outside world and the objective-psychic world of the Court, which overlaps and is resident in the midst of the normal world.

One great cause of difficulty and disorientation for the accused is the way in which the world is increasingly transformed by the Court, so that it is impossible for him to distinguish between what belongs to the objective-psychic world of the Court and what to the normal outside world. More and more the "normal" world becomes the world of the Court and the objective-psychic dimension appears within it, yet in spite of this the world remains the world. The objective-psychic dimension is to be found in the background of all human beings and many of them suspect its existence or actually know about it; naturally, then, as the Trial progresses the objective-psychic dimension will also begin to be discernible in the background of so-called normal people who are not identifiable as "officials," and in this way they reveal that they too belong to the Court and play their part in the Trial. This shifting of levels and uncertainty about the frame of reference is the cause of one of the most tormenting enigmas of the Trial, not least, of course, to the accused person.

K.'s second encounter with the Whipper situation culminates in a surprisingly desperate outburst: "At once K. slammed the door shut and then beat on it with his fists, as if that would shut it more securely. He ran almost weeping to the clerks."

What we have here is more than a failure, it is a genuine "catastrophe reaction." K. had really been hounded by the Whipper scene; his rationalization that he was innocent had evidently not convinced him, strange thoughts of sacrifice had preyed on his mind and had made him feel insecure. It was only the knowledge that this equivocal situation now lay finally behind him that had enabled him to repress it all. But now, when he suddenly found himself faced with the same situation once again, he broke down; for his reaction was in effect a collapse. To intervene responsibly with total commitment—or to become guilty: these were the alternatives he found himself confronted with. And both of them signified the collapse of his position. The blind fury of his reaction, when he shut his eyes, refused to look, and barricaded the door, does not represent a valid way out of the difficulty. K. is really trying to evade the necessity for a decision; yet he himself observes that the slamming of the door is itself a decision. The knowledge that he has been compelled to make a decision is what actually precipitates the release of his affect.

Evidence of this knowledge of K's is to be found in his terror, which forces him, the proud one, to seek the company of his clerks, and also in his desperate equivocal cry, "Clear the storeroom out, can't you? We're being smothered in dirt!" This shout is as helpless and as cognizant of his own guilt as his earlier declaration to Frau Grubach: "If you want to keep your house respectable you'll have to begin by giving me notice."

When K. cries out, "We're being smothered in dirt," this means that he can feel the Trial rising within him and is afraid of being smothered by it; but it also means that it is his own dirt in which he is being smothered. Yet precisely this dreamlike condensation of meanings contains a hint that there is something inside him which knows that these two things are really identical. It is not simply that this "rising" of the Trial is dependent on the rising of feelings of guilt and dirt within K. The Trial simply is this rising of guilt, it is K.'s inner state of erosion by guilt. In the last analysis this identity explains the meaning of the statement that the authorities who conduct the Trial are drawn towards the guilty but never go hunting for them in the populace.

It is extremely significant that the "objective" or juridical side of the Trial gradually becomes clearer, and that we are given a more and more comprehensive picture of the judges, the defense, the conduct of the Trial, the nature of the proceedings, etc.

Side by side with this process of the "unveiling" of the Court, K.'s own Trial is gaining ground on all sides. The nature of this expansion will be our next concern.

K.'s collapse after the repetition of the whipping scene marks a stage in this process of development. Gradually, K.'s attitude to the Trial changes. This change is apparent to outside observers, as we can clearly gauge from its effect on his uncle, who says, "Your attitude doesn't please me at all, that isn't how an innocent man behaves if he's still in his senses," and "Looking at you, one would almost believe the old saying: 'Cases of that kind are always lost.'"

K.'s behavior towards his uncle and towards Leni is dictated by a steadily increasing sense of insecurity, which he is no longer able to conceal, even outwardly, by his apparently calm, indifferent, and objective manner. Though he does say, "No case is won by getting excited," it becomes more and more of an effort for him to preserve his composure. He tells Leni, "Probably I brood far too little over my case," but not long afterwards, we read, "The thought of his case never left him now" and "The contempt which he had once felt for the case was no longer justified. . . . In short, he hardly had the choice now to accept the trial or reject it, he was in the middle of it and must fend for himself. To give in to fatigue would be dangerous."

Beyond all forebodings and half-knowledge, all feelings of fear and insecurity, K.'s conscious mind has now at last fallen under the spell of the Trial; his conscious attitude has also undergone a fundamental change. He has recognized the gravity and the menace of the Trial and he no longer thinks of it as a joke or only as something that can be dealt with casually or in a few moments.

In spite of this, however, K.'s moral evaluation of the Trial remains unaltered; and above all, his moral estimate of himself has not changed in the slightest degree. It is true that the Trial is something which has to be reckoned with, but his relationship to it is purely external; it has nothing to do with K. himself, let alone with his essential inner being.

"Above all . . . it was essential that he should eliminate from his mind the idea of possible guilt. There was no such guilt. This legal action was nothing more than a business deal." So K. tries over and over to fight his way through the Trial by enlisting allies, by "making arrangements" and similar measures. For him it is a battle: he gradually sees the good name of his family, his professional position, his private personal relationships, and in fact his entire bourgeois existence becoming dependent on the course of the Trial; yet he persists undeviatingly in his "heroic" attitude. "The Court would encounter for once an accused man who knew how to stick up for his rights."

In reality, however, something quite different happens. The Trial gradually takes hold of K.'s world and begins to expand. It has already encroached on his business and his family; the whole world knows about K.'s Trial, it is simply ubiquitous. At the same time something extraordinary happens to K. himself.

"What an obstacle had suddenly arisen to block K.'s career!" In this sentence a decisive change in the course of the Trial is epitomized. The Trial is beginning to devour K.'s life.

K. is obliged to draw up a plea, an account of his whole life down to the smallest actions and accidents, an "almost interminable labor." But he no longer defends himself against this necessity. "Today K. was no longer hampered by feelings of shame. The plea simply had to be drawn up. If he could find no time for it in his office, which seemed very probable, then he must draft it . . . by night. And if his nights were not enough, then he must ask for furlough." And all this although K. knew that "the completion of this plea was a sheer impossibility."

K. takes the view that he can no longer entrust his defense to anybody else, he must "put himself completely in the power of the Court, at least for the time being," since "while his case was unfolding itself . . . was he to devote his attention to the affairs of the Bank?" All at once K. was forced by the inner development of the Trial to face the necessity of "cutting himself off from every activity." Suddenly it becomes clear that K. is now a prisoner under observation.

This inner development of the Trial is the real cause of all its "unfolding" and "expansion." Intervention from outside by "Institutions of the Court" is never responsible for initiating development; the motive power is always

supplied by the development of the Trial itself, which
may best be compared with the progress of a disease.
This inner development of the Trial culminates in the
increasing isolation of K., and in a more and more
marked separation between himself and the "real" world.
There is a tremendous tenacity of purpose in the proceedings, which started with K.'s arrest; and now for the
first time the real nature of this arrest becomes apparent:
it does literally involve a deprivation of freedom. The
statement, "You are under arrest, nothing more," to
which K. felt he was entitled to react with such insolent
levity, is now revealed in all its uncanny ambiguity.
After the Inspector said, "You are under arrest, certainly,
but that need not hinder you from going about your
business. You won't be hampered in carrying on in the
ordinary course of your life," his statement turned out to
be the typical remark of a minor official. Factually, it is
correct; and no exception can be taken to it on this level.
But in its essential meaning we could just as well say that
this statement is entirely mistaken. And yet we should
be by no means justified in blaming the official. His statement is correct, but he himself is unaware; he has no
idea of the real function of the arrest.

It is only gradually, as the Trial proceeds, that the
full significance of the arrest becomes apparent. And
then our hypothesis about K.'s being "a prisoner under
observation" is confirmed by the tradesman, Block, who
has also been put on trial.

He himself describes how the inner development of
his Trial is leading him away from the "real" life of the
outside world: "That's why I've spent every penny I

possess on this case. For instance, I've drawn all the money out of my business; my business offices once filled nearly a whole floor of the building, where now I need only a small back room and an assistant clerk." His life with Advocate Huld is entirely the existence of a prisoner; his room is "a low-roofed windowless chamber which was completely filled by a narrow bed."

In glaring contrast to the incessant and indefatigable efforts of Block is K.'s negligence. As a result of this weakness K. is constantly making mistakes at which he himself is subsequently shocked. The haste and abruptness of his decisions—whether he is rushing off to see Titorelli, dismissing the Advocate, or surrendering to Leni—show a total lack of thought and consideration and contradict the principle he himself had formulated: "To be always forearmed, never to let himself be caught napping."

It is clear that the catastrophe which seized K. when the Whipper scene was repeated is steadily increasing its hold on him; it is more and more obvious that he has lost his way. We read that "the thought of his case never left him now." And shortly afterwards he tells the Advocate, "I was never so plagued by my case in earlier days as since engaging you to be my Advocate" and speaks of himself as a man who feels the Trial "secretly encroaching upon him and literally touching him to the quick."

The way in which K. now lets everything drop, his exhaustion and his rapidly mounting defeatism almost suggest the growth in him of a drive for self-annihilation. The question, "But was not K. abandoning more than was absolutely needful?" can only be understood in this sense.

This symptom is closely connected with K.'s growing knowledge of the Trial and with the increasing insight of his "other part" as compared with his ego, whose position is becoming steadily weaker. The ego now feels the hopelessness of its resistance. This is the source of K.'s defeatism; on the other hand his conscious mind is becoming increasingly aware of the knowledge of his transpersonality.

Two small pointers are particularly revealing in this connection. K. is thinking about the inner development of the Trial, its disastrous consequences and the torment of his split existence, compelled as he is to function as a bank official and an accused man at one and the same time. Suddenly, he asks himself, "Does it not look like a kind of torture sanctioned by the Court, arising from his case and concomitant with it?" This question, which sees the entire context at a single moment and comprehends the whole Trial and its legality, shows us how much K.'s conscious mind already "knows" and how passionately K. has been compelled to come to terms with the knowledge of his transpersonal side.

Still more significant is another of K.'s thoughts. K. is ruminating about the problem of his defense by the Advocate, and he wonders why the Advocate has not interrogated him. How on earth can anyone defend him without first having interrogated him? And then he thinks, "To ask questions was surely the main thing? Indeed K. felt that he himself could draw up all the necessary questions."

We learn that the difficulty experienced by the Advocate and in fact by a defense counsel of any kind is simply that they do not know the charge. They possess no factual information, and are therefore obliged to act purely formally and are not in a position to ask any questions. K. on the other hand "felt that he himself could draw up all the necessary questions." He in fact is the only person who is properly informed about the points of the charge, since the Interrogation Commission has its seat in K. himself. It is precisely because K. is the only person who knows about the charge and about what is at stake that he is dissatisfied with the uncertainty of the Advocate and with the measures taken by him. It is for this reason that all the accused have so many advocates—Block for example has seven! Only they "know" that nothing is really done to promote their defense, since the Trial takes its course irresistibly within themselves.

It is this knowledge which lies behind K.'s thoughts; and it is the realization that this is so which carries us straight to the heart of the "legal position" of the Trial itself.

Occasional communications from subordinate members of the staff had supplied K. with information about the procedure, the Trial, the judges, and the Law. Yet all the essentials remained shrouded in darkness; only the development of the Trial itself, as K. had been obliged to experience it in his own person, made it possible to gain some measure of insight.

K.'s suspicion that there was a great organization at work behind the Trial seemed to be substantiated. The existence of a body of officials with unspecified powers had been revealed; moreover, the institution of the Court played a significant though covert role in the popular imagination. Proverbs, widely held opinions, and superstitions alluded to the secret fact of its existence.

K. himself is bewildered and becomes more and more depressed and astonished when he finds that everyone with whom he comes into contact seems to know about the Court and even about his own Trial. This process sets in at the moment before his arrest, when the old lady opposite "peers at him with a curiosity unusual even for her," and it continues, via the uncle who travels up from the country to see him, to the foreign manufacturer who gives him advice and recommendations about his case. Everyone with whom K. comes into contact knows about the Trial and is connected with it. It is as if the disease of the Trial within K. attacks the world around him like an infection, so that he can no longer escape the atmosphere of the Court, and finally his whole existence is more and more narrowly encompassed and confined by a world that *is* the Court and the Trial.

When the manufacturer and the Deputy Manager are talking to each other about business, "it seemed to K. as though two giants of enormous size were bargaining above his head for himself. Slowly, lifting his eyes as far as he dared, he peered up to see what they were about, then picked up one of the documents from the desk at random, laid it flat on his open palm, and gradually raised it, rising himself with it, to their level. In doing so he had no definite purpose, but merely acted with the feeling that this was how he would have to act when he had finished the great task of drawing up the plea which

was completely to acquit him." And when the Deputy
Manager does not even read the paper through and says,
"Thanks, I know all that already" ("For anything that
seemed important to the Assessor was unimportant to
him"), then behind this scene, for anyone who, like K.,
is already aware of the questionable efficacy of pleas and
of the efforts of the Defense, there shimmers a demonic
and fateful significance. In this case, however, it is also
quite conceivable that a scene which is in itself unimportant may be invested with this unearthly shimmer by
K.'s own fantasy, pregnant as it is with the imagery of
the Trial.

All the more striking, in that case, is Titorelli's remark,
later on, when he tells K. that "everything belongs to
the Court"—a remark which is given special significance
by K.'s dismissive reply: "That's something I hadn't
noticed." Usually, what K. hasn't noticed turns out to be
the crucial consideration—and the Court, at least in the
opinion of many, is everywhere objectively present, and
in any case its existence is independent of K. as a perceiv-
ing subject. But if, in the end, it turns out that everyone
—including Fräulein Bürstner, the girls on Titorelli's
staircase, and cousin Erna—does belong to the Court,
and that the circles in which they live only surround the
High Authority at greater or lesser intervals, then we
find ourselves confronted, more insistently than before,
with a phenomenon which is a constant source of per-
plexity. If everyone belongs to the Court, why is it that
no one knows anything whatever about it?

It is not perhaps surprising that people who do not
officially belong to the Court—the private citizens, as we

might call them—should know nothing about its institutions, except possibly in the broadest general terms. In their case the problem would be how they can be said to belong to the Court at all—how, for example, the Court can become "transparent" in such figures as the Deputy Manager and the manufacturer. But the position is quite different with those who belong to the Court officially—from the warders to the Examining Magistrates and those higher up in the scale. What is the meaning of "ignorance" in their case and how can that be explained?

The warders and the Law Court Attendant and his wife are such subordinate employees that an insight into the real nature of the institutions of the Court cannot either be expected or required of them. They are purely executive functionaries, and it is in fact an essential part of their duties that they should *not* worry their minds any further about them. Their dullness reinforces their "partial private freedom." The further removed they are from the central authority, and the less their whole being is permeated by it, the more they are "private citizens," who display the qualities of common humanity and whose behavior is unofficial. These, then, are the so-called "gaps of the Court."

Yet even among such low-grade officials there are two features which strike our attention. These subordinate officers are responsible for the consequences of their actions and are subject to the absolute authority of the Court, as was effectively demonstrated in the Whipping chapter. They too take the utmost pains in the performance of their official duties. They are most conscientious servants of the Court and they have a profound insight into the limits of their status. For example, the unshakable faith of the warders in the wisdom of the high authorities in whose service they are engaged makes it possible even for these most humble employees of the Court to obtain naive but profound insights into the nature of the proceedings and of the judicial authorities.

The conversation of the warders with K. in Chapter 1 is full of insights of this kind. In fact, from the vantage point of a later stage of the Trial, we can see that K. had been given all the information he needed for the conduct of his case at the time of his original arrest; it was his "superiority" which had prevented him from listening to it.

The mere fact that they belonged to the Court seems to have made this source of insight available to the warders, though they are, of course, inferior in rank even to low-grade clerks.

Did we not start out, only a moment ago, from the proposition that even the higher officials were "ignorant," and are we not now asserting the precise opposite?

A partial knowledge of generalities and of the framework of the proceedings in the widest sense exists side by side with a complete lack of information about the details of particular cases. That is the essential consideration. Even the warders say, "Our officials . . . never go hunting for crime in the populace, but, as the Law decrees, are drawn towards the guilty and must then send out us warders. That is the Law. How could there be a mistake in that?" But when it is a matter of K.'s own

Trial, the Inspector says, "You are under arrest, certainly, more than that I do not know." And this continues to be the case throughout. K. is given a great deal of information, some of which is most comprehensive, but when it comes to the progress of his own Trial, nobody possesses any factual information whatever. The clearest statement is to be found in Advocate Huld's remarks about the officials: "The ranks of officials in this judiciary system mounted endlessly, so that not even adepts could survey the hierarchy as a whole. And the proceedings of the Courts were generally kept secret from subordinate officials, consequently they could hardly ever quite follow in their further progress the cases on which they had worked; any particular case thus appeared in their circle of jurisdiction often without their knowing whence it came, and passed from it they knew not whither. . . . They were forced to restrict themselves to that stage of the case which was prescribed for them by their Law, and as for what followed, in other words the results of their own work, they generally knew less about it than the Defense, which as a rule remained in touch with the accused almost to the end of the case." This principle of secrecy, according to which each particular official only bore a partial responsibility, restricted to that section of the case which had been prescribed for him, actually makes possible the impartiality of the proceedings. The partial private freedom of the individual functionaries of the Court can be permitted for the simple reason that all opportunities for exerting any real influence have been effectively removed from them. Thus, although justice is not guaranteed, it is true

53

to say that the possibility of injustice arising out of the action of the functionaries has in practice been excluded.

The result is a remarkable state of affairs. On the one hand, the officials are incredibly industrious in the performance of their responsible tasks; even the wife of the Law Court Attendant confirmed this and the Advocate also remarked, "How seriously these gentlemen took their vocation and how deeply they were plunged into despair when they came upon obstacles which the nature of things kept them from overcoming." On the other hand, this official impartiality contrasted with a private freedom of an altogether different kind. The essential characteristic here is a vanity which is repeatedly stressed by the author and which borders on the grotesque. This vanity is tolerated and recognized by the high authorities. It is clear from Titorelli's observations that the judges were given permission to get themselves painted "like that," where "like that" means on high seats which do not exist, with a statue of Justice at the back of each chair and a gloriole around the head.

Even more typical than this toleration is the way in which it is restricted at the same time. Each judge is given precise instructions as to how he may have his portrait painted. The Court is concerned to award a form of compensation to its functionaries, on whom the principle of the secrecy of the proceedings imposes a great deal of self-denial. But this toleration and support of private vanity is immediately integrated into the great organization. The vanity points to something greater that lies beyond. To be a functionary of the great organization of the Court is a dignity which raises the individual

above himself. In their capacity as functionaries of the
Court, the judges are no longer private persons. The le-
gally regulated gradation of the "promotions," the high
seats, and the glorioles around their heads are only an
expression of transpersonality in its more or less wide-
ranging manifestations.

The irritability, vindictiveness, and unpredictability
mentioned by Advocate Huld are quite a different matter. If we sum up the total effect of all the examples
mentioned by the Advocate, we shall finally arrive at
the conclusion that these very "human-all-too-human"
qualities of the officials—their moods, etc.—make the exercise of undue influence impossible, or at any rate so un-
certain that it can be discounted. This is especially true
when, for example, the definite promise of a judge that he
will do something on behalf of the Defense provides no
guarantee that he will not issue a statement of the Court
to the opposite effect immediately afterwards. This prevents the exercise of undue influence on the proceedings
of the Court, all the more so since the influence of an
individual functionary is exceedingly small in any case.
Under the same judiciary system, individual judges are
only permitted to see sections of any given case. The
result is that "their remoteness kept the officials from being in touch with everyday life" and "since they were
confined day and night to the workings of their judicial
system, they did not have any right understanding of
human relations." Even if this was "indispensable," the
very fact did guarantee an impersonal treatment of the
individual case.

At this point something must be said about the difficult problem of the officials of the Court. We have encountered two phenomena in this connection: the first was the private freedom of the officials and the second their transpersonality. To the extent that they do not constitute "service," i.e., the carrying out of the work of the Court, human conduct and life belong to the sphere of "private freedom." On the other hand, that part of their personality which is enlisted in the service of the Trans is "transpersonality." But we realize now that K., too—and in fact every human being—is actually made up of a duality of this kind. What is it, then, that makes an official an official? In what way do officials differ from other people?

As it progressed, the Trial had steadily expanded its range, so that finally the entire world belonged to it and everyone became an official for K., i.e., everyone performed a function of the Court in relation to him. What made this possible was the fact that at any given moment the Trans might become visible behind the world of ordinary reality, and the transpersonality behind the private personality of the individual human being. This possibility, however, was independent of the conscious mind of the individual concerned; it depended solely on the progress of the Trial within K. As the objective-psychic dimension moves closer to K. in its manifestation as the Court and his knowledge of it increases, so, at the same time, "outside" himself, the "normal" world becomes transparent to him, since in it, too, the objective-psychic dimension of the Court becomes manifest. But the external hierarchy of this Court is determined by the degree of its own Self-consciousness, i.e., of its consciousness of its own transpersonality.

People who know nothing at all about the Trans and are in fact only its blind tools (since the Trans speaks through them to K. as it speaks, e.g., through the Deputy Manager, K.'s uncle, Frau Grubach, etc.) are not initially identified as functionaries. They are not rendering any service of which they are cognizant. They do not know that they are functionaries at all. As consciousness of the transpersonality progresses, and with it, of course, consciousness of the nature of the Trans, office and rank ascend in scale. The wife of the Law Court Attendant already "knows" about the Trans. When she allows herself to be misused by the law student or by officials of the Court she is submitting to the Trans. Admittedly, she has very little consciousness indeed; she has an urge to serve rather than a function of service; yet the fact remains that as a result of it she deserts K. without hesitation. (We may note here that the attitude of women to the Trans plays a particularly large and important part in the Commentary on the Castle.) In ascending order we witness the same phenomenon with the warders, the whippers, the girl in the Law Court offices, and finally in the hierarchy of the officials. Even at the lowest level we find a consciousness of service that perfectly corresponds with the knowledge of the transpersonality possessed by the functionary concerned. The more anyone knows of the Trans, the less partial, private freedom he possesses and the more he *is* the service that he renders. A good example of this is the officer from the penal colony. In fact, if we wished to describe the ascending hierarchy of the Court, we could say that it was a succession of stages which represent growing knowledge of the transpersonality and growing conscious service of the Trans.

When it comes to the lower authorities, however, which are the only ones with whom K. comes into contact, the life of the officials is always involved in a piquant and often embarrassing state of private freedom, which, however, as we have already seen, is powerless to affect the real course of events, and is in fact entirely segregated from it. We have already emphasized the way in which their objective appearance in visible form depends on K.'s subjective Trial. This coincidence of objective and subjective, "normal world" and "world of the Court," leads in K.'s instance to a process of concretization in the form of an intermediate reality. The relationship of the officials to the Court, the connection between their transpersonality and the Trans, and the exclusion of private independence bring us face to face with the situation of the Defense. We notice that the good personal relations between Advocate Huld and the higher officials ("of subordinate rank, naturally") represent a very small factor in the Defense and that their significance could be said to be virtually nil. And when Huld concludes that "the very lowest grade of the Court organization was by no means perfect and contained venal and corruptible elements, whereby to some extent a breach was made in the watertight system of justice," and that this was where petty advocates tried to push their way in—ultimately, however, without success—then we can see that the difference between him and these petty advocates was not very great. Block's statement, too, that Advocate Huld was one of the minor advocates confirms this conclusion. The entire effort of the Defense—with the solitary exception of the "great advocates"—is an attempt, foredoomed to failure from the outset, to infiltrate the structure of the great organization. As Huld himself admits, "The Defense was not actually countenanced by the Law, but only tolerated, and there were differences of opinion on that point. Therefore, none of the advocates was recognized by the Court." However, the resulting "bad treatment" of the advocates was not without justification. The authorities wished to discourage defending counsel as much as possible; the whole onus of the Defense must be laid on the accused himself. Huld mentions that the Defense is not even informed about the nature of the charge, and in this connection we may be struck by the remarkable fact, which at first sight appears completely unintelligible, that there is not a single mention of a charge in the entire course of the Trial. K. is simply arrested. There is a possibility that he may be interrogated by the Examining Magistrate, but we hear nothing about an indictment. We are told, it is true, that the proceedings are to a large extent kept secret, even from the accused, but as we have already observed, K. was apparently the only person who knew anything about the points of the indictment. That is only another way of expressing the fact that the indictment was a happening within K. himself.

But is not Titorelli's statement about "ostensible acquittal" and "indefinite postponement" contradicted if we assume that the efforts of the Defense are an attempt (condemned to failure) to infiltrate the gaps in the great organization? Are not these in fact examples of successes achieved by the Defense as a result of the exploitation of personal relationships?

"Intense concentration at long intervals" with the object of influencing the Judges will result in the circulation of an "affidavit" among them, and this in turn will be followed by an "ostensible acquittal." In fact, however, only the highest Court, which is inaccessible to all, possesses the right of acquittal, not the lower Judges. Thus it is possible for an accused man who has just left the Court after his acquittal to go straight home and find officers already waiting to arrest him again. And this circle can be repeated indefinitely; ostensible acquittal achieves nothing, except that the affidavit is added to the charge, together with a record of the acquittal and the grounds for granting it. No real change, therefore, let alone a termination of the Trial, is achieved by this method.

The position with "indefinite postponement" is similar. Here the effort is directed at preventing the case from ever getting any further than its first stages. This is less taxing to the accused but means a steady strain. Here too the charge always remains open. The accused lives in a constant state of "Trial alertness," of the kind we have witnessed in the case of K. and also of Block, who succeeded in "carrying his burden" for more than five years. The anxiety about the Trial and also the absorption in it (the so-called "imprisonment on remand") continue to exist in both these forms of "success."

All these detours and escapes can be cut off at any

moment by an intervention of the high authorities which "took the case out of the hands" of the advocates. "The case had simply reached the stage where further assistance was ruled out . . . where even the accused was beyond the reach of an Advocate." All the pleas were in this case returned to the Advocate, "because in the new stage of the process they were not admitted as relevant; they were mere wastepaper." This withdrawal of the case throws a particularly clear light on the illusory activity of the Defense; in point of fact, it is identical with postponement and ostensible acquittal.

Titorelli summarizes its significance as follows: "Both methods have this in common, that they save the accused from coming up for sentence," and K. answers, in a low voice, as if embarrassed by his own perspicacity, "But they also prevent an actual acquittal." "You have grasped the kernel of the matter," Titorelli replies immediately.

Ultimately, the Defense turns out to be impotent, and even K. notices this: "The repeated mention of his innocence was already making K. impatient. At moments it seemed to him as if the painter was assuming that K.'s case was bound to turn out well and that on these terms his own help would be worth having." This suspicion of K.'s is confirmed by Advocate Huld's despairing admission that in dark hours "you thought you had achieved nothing at all . . . it seemed to you that only the cases predestined from the start to succeed came to a good end, which they would have reached in any event without an Advocate's help."

However, the impossibility of a Defense that took the form of the exercise of influence by direct or indirect means is not the only way in which the "inescapability" of the Trial makes itself evident.

Right at the beginning we read that "the high authorities . . . before they would order such an arrest as this must be quite well informed about the reasons for the arrest and the person of the prisoner. There can be no mistake about that." K. himself, in the course of his increasingly doubtful affirmation of his innocence, happens to mention that "they all agree on one thing, that charges are never made frivolously, and that the Court, once it has brought a charge against someone, is firmly convinced of the guilt of the accused and can be dislodged from that conviction only with the greatest difficulty." "Difficulty!" cries the painter. "Never can the Court be dislodged from that conviction. If I were to paint all the Judges in a row on one canvas and you were to plead your case before it, you would have more hope of success than before the actual Court." " 'I see,' said K. to himself, forgetting that he merely wished to probe the painter."

This "I see" of K.'s, which is spoken to himself, is like his shocked surprise when he is told about the futility of ostensible acquittal: it confirms the absolute inescapability of the Trial. He is in fact completely surrounded, without any possibility of escape. There is no way he can evade the Trial, nowhere he can break out of it; the Court is a pack of hounds that yelps around him every second of his existence—and suddenly the cruel, uncanny symbol which he has just glimpsed lights up to an unearthly triumphal clarity. The goddess of the chase is the goddess of victory—and her name is—Justice! For an instant the similarity of the Trial to Greek tragedy becomes luminous—the hunting of the guilty by Justice, by the Erinyes, who pant upon his heels and hound him to his death. K.'s desperate and agonizing fear, his shivering, quavering, and frenzied attempts—all abortive—to rescue himself are nothing but the hopeless struggles of a deer to elude its pursuers; and we read, "The hounds are still playing in the farmstead, but the deer will not elude them, however wildly it chases through the forests."

Without K. being aware of this himself, the discerning judgment expressed by the accused Block does in fact apply to his own life: "There is an old maxim: people under suspicion are better moving than at rest, since at rest they may be sitting in the balance without knowing it, being weighed together with their sins."

But if a vengeful and pitiless foe hunts down the accused, what has that to do with justice? And what are we to think of a Court which acknowledges no acquittals? Is not K. right when he says, "A single executioner could do all that is needed," since after all the legends of acquittals in earlier times are of no more practical importance to an accused man than the existence of inaccessible "Great Advocates."

The fundamental reality is and always remains that the Trial has its basis of activity within K., that K.'s development is the Trial's own development, which is in fact the development of the consciousness of guilt in K. K.'s knowledge of the problems which beset the Defense, his knowledge of the charge and of his own tormenting suspicion, which makes it seem more and more probable to him that the Court "will conjure up, out of nothing, an enormous fabric of guilt," makes it impossible for the Defense to achieve any kind of success.

Since the real heart of the Trial is its inner development within K., it follows that any external approach through the gaps in the Court or by way of "other people" is fruitless and can never lead to an acquittal, but only at the best to "ostensible acquittals" or to completely insignificant postponements. That is the meaning of Block's statement: "Combined action against the Court is impossible. Each 'case is judged on its own merits, the Court is very conscientious about that."

The very fact that the fulcrum of the Trial is situated within forms a frozen empty space of isolation around the accused man. Even in a world full of people who are eager to help, no one can break through to him. As the Trial gains ground his loneliness increases. The Trial takes hold of the entire world and thrusts itself more and more inexorably between him and the reality of his fellow human beings. This isolation, which is nothing less than the deep-rooted reality of the Trial in the accused, is also responsible for the "secrecy of the proceedings," and explains why no official has any specific information about the procedure of the Trial. The fact that the essential proceedings of the Trial are also kept secret from the accused man himself only proves that he, too, in the truest sense of the word does not know what is happening to and in himself. Yet in spite of this it is he himself who is secretly directing the course of the Trial, since the Court does not seek out guilt but is attracted by it—a point, incidentally, which should specially be stressed in view of the inexorability of the Trial. The guilt of the accused is the primary factor. The Court is, as it were, at the service of the accused; it is not free, it is subject to the Law. Now, too, we can understand why we are told, "To have a case of this kind is to have lost it already," and why the Court acknowledges no acquittal. No frivolous charges are made. Guilt cries out to the Court. There is no mistake in that. The loneliness of the accused man is a concomitant of his guilt, for he is and remains alone with it. Nobody can take it away from him, for the Court and the Trial and the inner development of the Trial are something within himself. His loneliness is only a symptom of the Trial, and like all the other symptoms of the Trial it also has a positive side, since it aims at helping the accused finally to look within. As the warder said at the beginning, "Think less about us and about what is going to happen to you, think more about yourself instead." It is a simple and inexorable matter of fact that only the accused can help himself, no one else.

Actually, the only remedies against the Trial are either innocence (but no innocent man is ever involved in a Trial) or confession. As Leni tells K., "You can't put up a resistance against this Court, you must admit your fault. Make your confession at the first chance you get. Until you do that, there's no possibility of getting out of their clutches, none at all." Confession, involving insight into your own guilt, is the real meaning of the Trial. The punishment is to a large extent included in the Trial, because, as we learn later on, "the proceedings gradually merge into the verdict." We could say that imprisonment on remand is included in the sentence, and if we think of the existence endured by the accused Block, we shall understand that conducting the Trial, being sentenced, and paying the penalty are one and the same thing, and that once again the decisive consideration is the absence of any form of external constraint on Block. He acts entirely of his own free will; he himself sentences and punishes himself. To conduct your own Trial means at the same time to execute it on your own person.

But what is the guilt of the accused? What is K.'s guilt? Here too we are given no direct information; in fact we receive very little direct information about the Trial as a whole. Yet something quite basic about K.'s guilt can be stated with a degree of confidence.

One of K.'s most essential characteristics is his incapacity for human relationships, which is based on an egoism of a most deep-rooted kind. His behavior towards the women and the warders, and later on towards his uncle, the Advocate, Leni, Block, and in fact everyone with whom he comes into contact betrays the same unswerving, callous, and yet almost natural attitude that is typical of the threatened egoist. This feature becomes more and more obvious as the Trial continues (in total contrast, e.g., to the honest efforts made by Block), and it is perhaps most blatantly exposed in K.'s dismissal of the Advocate.

The Advocate has laid bare to K. his whole way of life, this miserable existence of a man who longs in vain to help others, and he has actually included a personal confession in which he tells K., "Your uncle is a friend of mine, and I've grown fond of you, too, in the course of

time. I admit it freely. It's nothing to be ashamed of."
Yet K.'s sole reaction is that he finds this outburst of the
old man's sentimental and "most unwelcome." We shall
not repeat our enumeration of the qualities that demonstrate the hardened egoism of K.; we shall only quote a
single sentence which may perhaps indicate that the basic
fact of his own guilt had not entirely escaped K.'s consciousness: "The contempt which he had once felt for the
case was no longer justified. Had he stood alone in the
world he could easily have ridiculed the whole affair,
though it was also certain that in that event it could
never have arisen at all."

If it is true that K.'s basic guilt is to be found in his
failure to relate adequately to his fellow human beings,
then it is certainly no accident that the events of his own
Trial should take place in the cruelest and most inexorable solitude. The ancient law of Justice, "An eye for an
eye and a tooth for a tooth," here returns in a new form:
"The man who leaves others alone will himself be left
alone." But what makes this "being left alone" so eerie
and so overpowering is the fact that K. is surrounded by
a world that wishes, but is unable, to help him. It recoils
from the pitiless wall of the Law which surrounds him
as a result of his own guilt. K. in fact cannot be helped,
in spite of the friendliness of the proceedings and of
people generally, wherever he goes—whether this takes
the form of the "transgressions" of the lower functionaries or the efforts made by his uncle, Titorelli, or the girl
in the Law Court offices.

Two representatives of this friendly assistance play a
particularly prominent part—the Advocate Huld and

Leni, who represents the women. It is by no means impossible that the Advocate's conscientious devotion to his duties had actually made him ill in the first place, and that it was his efforts to "lift his client on his shoulders from the start and carry him bodily without once letting him down until the verdict is reached, and even beyond it" that had in fact resulted in his breakdown. The tragic part about such an existence is its inherent futility, together with the fact that, at least in dark hours, Huld is conscious of this state of affairs and realizes that his help is unnecessary or, more accurately, impossible. On one occasion Huld even goes so far as to say, "You could not positively deny . . . that your intervention might have sidetracked some cases which would have run quite well on the right lines had they been left alone." And that is quite correct, for in view of its illegality, reliance on the Defense is always a misguided path for the accused, a temptation to look outside instead of within, a temptation in fact to search for mediators in cases where the essential offering can only be yourself. So in spite of the best intentions the Advocate becomes something very like a seducer to the accused, and the same is true of Leni and the women. All these people tempt the accused to turn aside from the central object, which is the Trial itself. The very fact of seeking aid is a mistake in principle, which leads you away from the one thing needful. Yet genuine help does seem to lie hidden in Leni's love for the accused man. And apart from the true way of self-development *through* the Trial, the only sign of a way *out* of the Trial is perhaps to be found in a relationship with her. It is Leni who appeals to K. to make a confession, and her behavior towards Block also suggests that she is helping him along with his own Trial. This brings us to the remarkable phenomenon of the attractiveness of the accused men and of the love of Leni and the women for them. The "natural law" of the attractiveness of accused men is so obvious to those who are experienced in such matters that they can pick out "one after another all the accused men in the largest of crowds"; this is supposed to be due to "the . . . charge preferred against them that in some way enhances their attraction." In the opinion of the Advocate Huld this cannot be due to their guilt, "for—it behoves me to say this as an Advocate, at least—they aren't all guilty"; but clearly he is not convinced by his own line of argument. It is in fact their guilt, which is ultimately identical with the Trial itself, that constitutes the attractiveness of the accused.

Since the proceedings are a Trial which also takes place within the accused man himself and is even in a sense comparable with a disease, it is clear that this happening which completely changes him and his whole world, may also leave its mark "outwardly," on his facial appearance. The material available to us in *The Trial* is not in itself sufficient to enable us to explain why the accused men resemble one another in facial expression, and why this change in them should take the form of making them attractive. To provide an adequate reason for this, it will be necessary for us to refer to *In the Penal Colony*, a work whose relationship to *The Trial* will be discussed again, later on. There is a similar context in that novel where, although there is no mention of attractiveness, the change reported by the officer during the sixth hour of the execution in the machine seems very similar to the attractiveness of accused men who are undergoing a Trial. "It begins with the eyes and spreads from there. It is a look which might tempt a man to submit himself to the torment along with the condemned."

In the context of *In the Penal Colony*, the point is that the meaning of the agonizing execution dawns on the accused man during the sixth hour: the meaning is that *Justice is being done*. This change can also be seen on the face of the condemned man. Something similar, in fact most likely the same, happens in the Trial. Leni, too, feels the attractiveness of the accused men; she feels that both in them and on them Justice is being done, and she sees the change brought about in them by their growing consciousness of their guilt.

The attractiveness of the accused is in fact the breakthrough of their transpersonality, which becomes more and more unmistakable during the Trial. In the course of the proceedings, the ego or private personality becomes less and less important, while the transpersonality, the knowing foundation, takes over the leadership. But the transpersonality itself belongs to the Court, and it is an essential characteristic of Kafka's women that they always love, and are bound to love, anyone in whom they sense the presense of the Trans. Leni's love is really impersonal; in spite of all her wantonness and amorous behavior, it does transcend the personal dimension. And for this very reason she is also perhaps better qualified than anyone else to help the accused.

However, in contrast to the accused Block, who sup-

ports his defense by the advocates with immense eagerness and the most craven humility, K. dismisses his only
advocate. With an unerring instinct that betrays his increasing knowledge of the laws governing the Trial, he
makes no attempt to find another advocate, but determines to take the entire burden of the Defense onto his
own shoulders. This prompts the Advocate to tell him,
"I have an idea that what makes you so wrong-headed
not only in your judgment of my capacities but also in
your general behavior is the fact that you have been
treated too well, although you are an accused man, or
rather, more precisely, that you have been treated with
negligence, with apparent negligence." When he goes
on to say, "It's often safer to be in chains than to be
free," it almost seems as if the Court, in a dangerous and
malicious mood, is trying to lure K. into a trap.

This is a question we have already encountered once
before, on another level. We saw that the friendliness of
private people, which was one of the gaps in the judicial
system of the Court, at the same time constituted a
danger for the accused. This phenomenon does not arise
out of any kind of maliciousness; on the contrary, it
corresponds to a necessity, a law in fact, which has its
basis in the situation of the accused himself. Owing to
the fact that the accused cannot be helped "from outside," whatever is "outside" comes to be charged with
peril for him and does actually represent a kind of trap.
We must bear in mind that the situation of the accused
is by no means normal: it is in fact perverted in the extreme. K. is accused precisely because of his distorted
attitude to the world, and this embraces not only the

"normal world of human beings" but also the world of the objective psyche. The maxims that are the logical consequence of the law of "An eye for an eye and a tooth for a tooth" include not only "The man who leaves others alone will be left alone by others," but also necessarily—in fact the one involves the other—"The world becomes distorted to the man who has a distorted attitude towards the world." To such a man, love and friendship themselves become a peril and a trap. This, however, in no way implies that the world in itself is actually like that. The fact that it appears to the accused man in this light is one of those things which, we are told elsewhere, are "not true but necessary."

Human beings, insofar as they are human beings and "private" individuals, have no interest in supporting the Court. On the contrary, they try to help one another against the Court as if they were members of a secret alliance. They are all afraid of the Court, and among the lower officials this fact is not only obvious, it is openly admitted. Everyone is afraid of the overmastering power of the Trans, except insofar as he is conscious of the transpersonality within himself and knows he is identical with it—in which case he is an official, and a higher official at that. But the Court itself, that is the Trial, cannot be halted by any human being. The efforts of human beings to stop the Trial, in whose service they are engaged and which they themselves execute on the person of the accused, are fruitless. The Trial takes its course independently of them, running under its own power; its motor is within the accused himself.

No official, no authority, no institution "is" or consti-

tutes the Court. The Trans, represented in symbolic form
as Justice, the Goddess of Victory, and the Goddess of the
Chase, is higher than all of them. Officials and institutions are no more than half-conscious, half-unconscious,
or wholly unconscious executors of her purpose, and for
good or ill they have no effect on her unswerving course.
The only person who has any effect on that is the accused
man himself, for it is he who has invoked the Goddess
of Justice or, as we read in another passage, "The Court
makes no claims upon you. It receives you when you
come and relinquishes you when you go."

The only chance that the accused has of escaping from
the Court and the Trans is by way of the inner development provided by his Trial, which will lead him to his
own transpersonality and to the realization that the
Court is in himself, that he belongs to it and that he
himself is both official and Court.

This interdependence between the accused and the
Court finds expression not only in the passivity of the
proceedings (in the fact, e.g., that interference from outside by institutions of the Court never plays any part in
the Trial), but also in the individual form taken by
Trials of various kinds. The extreme difference between
K.'s fate and Block's, as exemplified in their respective
Trials, is illuminating in this context. Block is intensely
concerned and preoccupied by his Trial, he concentrates
his attention on it the whole time; and although, in spite
of all the anxiety and insecurity that every Trial entails,
he is apparently calm and collected, patient and unas-
suming, the Court confronts him from outside in the
form of a series of inquiries and torments. In spite of this,

he has already succeeded in prolonging his Trial (that is to say, in keeping alive) for five whole years. He, too, it seems, has not arrived at the stage of insight, confession, and redemption; his six advocates are sufficient evidence to the contrary. Yet his eagerness and his subservience may perhaps have the effect that he will only be condemned to "penal servitude for life." But it will be a long life, painfully dragged out to the end.

K.'s fate, on the other hand, is completely different. Here, too, we have the strange compensatory interaction between the "inner" and the "outer" dimensions, except that this time it works in the opposite direction. K.'s main concern is to repress the Trial as much as possible from his consciousness. He has refused to acknowledge the Interrogation Commission and has no further "outer" contact of any kind with the Court. All the more perilous and tormenting, however, is the way in which the Court now makes its appearance in the "inner" dimension, where it involves K. in a whole series of new inquiries. It is this rising tide of the inner Trial that is the characteristic feature of K.'s fate. And his type of development involves a quite specific peril, which also contrasts with Block's "penal servitude for life"—and that is the peril of "sudden execution." The apparent negligence of the proceedings only holds good in the outer dimension. Behind the façade of life which, again in contrast to Block's case, shows little sign of change, the process of undermining advances inexorably from within, pregnant with the hidden menace of some lethal catastrophe or explosion. K., once again, is aware of this menace, as he shows when he reflects that it is the policy of the Court "to lull the accused and keep him in a helpless state, in order suddenly to overpower him with the verdict."

The fact that this fear has an objective basis is proved not only by Huld's remark to Block, when he tells him that "you've read somewhere or other that a man's condemnation often comes by a chance word from some chance person at some odd time," but also by the actual outcome of K.'s Trial.

K.'s Trial will end in a sudden explosion, which penetrates and shatters the façade of negligence. That is exactly what K. is afraid of. Over and over again he tries to protect himself from himself, is terrified by his own complete unconsciousness of danger and afraid of sudden surprises. Then he believes that he can protect himself by an attitude of calmness and superiority and learns repeatedly that he cannot do this. Even then, he persuades himself that each failure is only a mistake. Yet on one occasion he actually experiences a sudden assault from within—and that signalizes the simultaneous breakthrough of terror inside himself. This happens when he collapses at the repetition of the Whipping scene. And this collapse, which was the first collapse of his façade, actually anticipates the final verdict. It is the first great crack in the front line of his existence, the emergence of that gradual change "from within" which Leni had recognized as the attractiveness of the accused.

Yet the fact that the result has to be an explosion is attributable—as we have seen and shall see over and over—exclusively to K. himself. If K. would open his mind to the reality growing within him and visibly transforming him more and more, the power of the transpersonality and, behind it, of the Trans, then there would have been confession, acquittal and, finally, redemption. Instead, though he constantly experiences and "knows" the power that is steadily growing inside him, he violently barricades his ego against it, and it is this that finally results in explosions and necessitates his own death.

A disposition of this kind, an ego with this kind of fixed hostility to the Trans, is ultimately incapable of living and is therefore exploded by its own "foundation." The justice of the Law of life wills it that way, the Trans has created the world in that pattern; the world simply "is" like that.

2

THE CATHEDRAL CHAPTER

The crucial importance of the Cathedral chapter is due to the fact that it contains the story entitled "Before the Law." This story, together with the ensuing discussion and interpretation, is the most illuminating summary of the happening of the Trial that we possess.

K. is suffering from persecution mania. He is constricted by a hideous circle of fear. He is afraid to accept any responsibility that involves leaving the bank on business or undertaking a short journey; yet for fear of betraying this fear, he does not dare to excuse himself from commissions of this kind, even if he is ill and would have had excellent reasons for refusing to leave the office.

K. seems to have completely lost the power to recognize reality for what it is. Inwardly, he is now so demoralized that in any conceivable combination of circumstances he is only capable of a single reaction—fear. The kinds of behavior exhibited by his fellow mortals have become simply irrelevant to him, since every attitude they adopt, every word they speak, can only mean one thing to him—menace. The Court is everywhere, but this implies that people are nowhere, the "normal" world of everyday life is nowhere—and peace and quiet are nowhere too.

K. is instructed to show the Cathedral to a visiting business friend. When he tells Leni this, she replies abruptly, "They're driving you!" but that only confirms K.'s general feeling that he is being persecuted. This going into the Cathedral plays by no means an insignificant part in the history of the Trial, as we realize from the chaplain's statement to K., "I had you called here to have a talk with you." K.'s answer, "I didn't know that. I came here to show an Italian round the Cathedral" meets with the simple reply, "That is a mere detail."

The ambiguity of what is happening becomes quite transparent here. The Interrogation Chamber, the Law Court offices, and the whipping room all belong to a world that is, as we have said, "resident in the midst" of normal reality and in which the subjective dimension of the psyche encounters the objective reality of the deep region of the Court. In this intermediate world there is a strange kind of double causality in which what is happening does not work itself out in normal reality but on the plane of the Court and of the Trial. The subterranean

chain of causality has a decisive influence on normal
reality, but only "in the long run"; at first it seems as if
the sphere of influence of the intermediate world is
banished every time the door is slammed.

The whipping scene had already shown us what the
logical consequence of this double causality might be.
An attitude that has no consequences on the plane of
outer reality, because what is happening is in point of
fact beyond the scope of the intervention of the person
concerned, can still involve guilt and can still, on the
plane of the Court, have incalculable results. The illusion
of free will is sufficient to create moral responsibility in
a man, and to make him accountable for all the consequences of his attitude. From the point of view of the
deep region of the Court, the effect of a man's attitude
on the plane of "normal reality" and on the causality of
the outside world is irrelevant, or at least may be irrelevant.

It is not disputed that K.'s purpose in visiting the
Cathedral is to show it to the Italian; on the plane of
outer existence the casual chain of events is unbroken
and contains no gaps. At the same time, this plane and
the secular causality that is appropriate to it are regarded
as "of secondary importance." The "real" causality is expressed in the chaplain's words, "I had you summoned
here."

This double nature of the world makes it possible for
an event that is not specially staged for a given person
to be nevertheless there "for him," since the Court tests
him and his attitude to that event. Quite independently
of the necessity of an event on the plane of outer reality,

this event is "intended for" a given person, particularly for him and at this particular moment, and is in fact teleologically aimed at him. The earthly, outer chain of events becomes the instrument of another series of happenings, which runs its course on a deeper plane of essential being. The events of the world become the vehicles for the intervention of the extramundane authority of the Court, which thus appears on the earthly plane. In this way it is possible for the deep authority of the Court to enter into a relationship with a man directly through the events of the world. No breach is made at any point in the causal chains of outer reality, but a space is created within the world's happenings in which a man's just and unjust actions can work out their effects. Yet here, too, nothing can be "proved"; no analysis of outer events can prove any intention or intervention of the "Trans," since it is only on the deeper plane of the Court that the other, second causality can be discerned at all. Yet it becomes clear that the "secular" causal series does not simply run its course side by side with the "real" causal series, but that the former is actually encompassed by the latter. It is not just a question of a different level of meaning or something of that kind, but of a genuine form of causality with its own series of effects, as we realize very clearly when we find that the Trial displays this causality of the Court as the real ruling principle of life itself, to which the whole of reality, including specifically outer reality, is subject.

K.'s behavior in the Cathedral only confirms what we already know about him. The obstinacy with which he does the wrong thing, in the face of all the warning hints

79

that are given him, his cowardice and the indecision which betrays him in all his attempts at escaping, are familiar characteristics. The freedom that was granted K. at the time of his arrest was "only real," "real only in an outward sense." As the Trial proceeded, K. had become less and less a "prisoner on remand" and more and more a "prisoner condemned to solitary confinement." Yet in harmony with the essential nature of the Trial, these penalties are imposed on him entirely from within; he is hounded by the development of the Trial within himself. So when the prison chaplain suddenly addresses him, it is impossible to avoid the suspicion that this is the clergyman's visit prescribed by law which is traditionally paid to a prisoner who has been condemned to death on the night before his execution, so that he can make his peace with the divine justice by confessing his guilt before he dies. The scene in the Cathedral takes place immediately before K.'s death; this seems to provide a definitive answer to the question as to the significance of the prison chaplain. There is, however, one sentence which almost gives the impression that we have not yet reached the ultimate stage of "the night before the prisoner's death." The prison chaplain tells K., "Your guilt is supposed, for the present at least, to have been proved." This phrase, "for the present at least," is curious and its implications are far-reaching. Since there is no doubt that we are intended to take the chaplain's words seriously in this context, we have to suppose he is saying or at least implying that there is a theoretical possibility that the Court's belief in K.'s guilt might be shown to be unfounded; moreover, this formulation almost sounds as if there was actually a disposition on the part of the Court to accept counter-evidence of K.'s innocence—and indeed that it was actually waiting for this evidence to be produced.

We have emphasized more than once that the primary concern of the trial is the guilt of the accused; this enabled us, for example, to understand why—according to Titorelli, at any rate—the Court acknowledges no acquittal. It is true that there are occasional references which suggest that a negative outcome of the Trial is not necessarily the only possibility. The most important of these is the mention by Titorelli of the legends of ancient court cases; in this passage he states that "actually the majority of them are about acquittals." Nothing definite can be said about this earlier period, if only because "the final decisions of the Court are never recorded," but Titorelli himself thinks that "they must have an element of truth in them," and that "they shouldn't be left entirely out of account." This fact implies, in the first place, a historical change in the evidence given by accused persons and, secondly, the possibility of an acquittal from the charge. At the same time the guilt of the accused remains the primum mobile of the Trial—and this principle, which is laid down in "the Law," is valid for all places and for all time. The change in the evidence, which has in fact deteriorated, because in modern times the accused have lost the ability to conduct a case that has actually started to the successful conclusion of an acquittal, will concern us later. What we have to explain, however, is how it can be said to be possible in principle to achieve an acquittal when guilt is presupposed by the very existence of a Trial.

We have already noticed that the penalty was included in the process of the Trial and that conducting a case, being condemned, and serving the sentence are essentially one and the same thing—or, as we expressed it with a slightly different emphasis, to conduct a Trial is to execute it on your own person. The prison chaplain's saying that "the verdict is not suddenly arrived at, the proceedings only gradually merge into the verdict," though it does not confirm the popular belief that a litigant always loses, may yet mean that a litigant is always already paying the penalty. The penalty corresponds to the guilt, which is presupposed by every Trial, but the severity of the penalty, which is the real sentence, has still to be determined.

The chaplain's statement is also the answer to K.'s complaints that the staff of the Court were prejudiced against him and that they were "influencing even outsiders." The transformation of the world by the Trial *into* the Trial, is already part of the execution of the sentence; in fact it "is" the penalty. Yet this state of affairs implies the possibility of an acquittal. In the Trial the accused is "revealed"; he shows the Court who he really is. That is why cross-questioning by the Examining Magistrate is considered unnecessary in K.'s case.

The focus of interest in the proceedings is never to be found where it seems to be. The basic error of the accused is precisely that they worry themselves about the Trial; they always imagine that certain specific "measures" are required. In reality the object of the proceedings is the accused's whole being, not his attitude to certain institutions. It is for this reason that the Court is to be found "everywhere," and that every human being "belongs to the Court," as K. learns from his own experience. The object of the proceedings is "life," the whole life of the accused, and "the Trial" only triggers off a particularly pronounced expression of the accused man's general attitude. The accused is a particular specimen of life, and there is nothing in him that differs in principle from the life of other human beings. The point is simply that this life is "under observation," that the eye of the Law, which is the Court, is "watching" this particular life.

Guilt is already there, at the beginning of the Trial; it is guilt that precipitates the "watching" of the Court. But during the Trial the accused still has a chance—to incur further guilt, quite apart from his initial guilt, just as he still has the power to establish his innocence, also apart from his initial guilt.

The accused does not know about the charge that has been brought against him; he has the chance to go on living, just like any other human being. This process of living under the eyes of the Court in a period of probation; the accused has a chance, even though he is aware that a charge has been leveled against him, to go on living "decently," which means, of course, in a *human* fashion. Not only does the Trial provide the accused with an opportunity to incur more and more new guilt, and by so doing to confirm his initial guilt in the eyes of the Court; it also gives him a chance to react in a way that is human and innocent. As we see it, the paradox of the possibility of acquittal in spite of initial guilt can, in fact, be resolved along these lines.

If it is true that the proceedings merge into the verdict and the execution of the penalty, and if the accused proves himself innocent by his conduct during the Trial, i.e., if he incurs no further guilt, then it is by no means unreasonable to suppose that at a certain stage in the Trial the initial guilt can be regarded as expiated and the final acquittal can take place. This means that the "great Advocates" could play a decisive part, since we now have an exceptional situation in which an Advocate might legitimately belong to the "Court." In that case the accused would need an Advocate, since he is guilty—otherwise he would not be involved in a Trial—but the Advocate is only satisfying the requirements of justice when he proves that the initial guilt has been expiated by the Trial itself, and that the time for an acquittal has come.

The fatalism that seemed to be the only possible attitude for those who were condemned to be accused has therefore actually turned out to be unjustified. The saying, "A litigant always loses," though it may be true empirically, is in principle false. It represents a widely held opinion, but even Titorelli shows his "displeasure" when K. is tempted to generalize from the painter's negative experiences and to interpret them as evidence for a universal law. If we wish to distinguish between the accused men of earlier times and those of today, we might do so by saying that nowadays the accused are no longer able to establish their innocence during the Trial and to avoid incurring further guilt. And if we take K. as an example, we can demonstrate, over and over again, that his behavior during the Trial constantly provides occasions which would justify bringing him to Trial in the first place. The "modernity" of the evidence given by the accused takes the form of an extraordinary resistance to insight. Even when the region of depth, the Trans, has already seized hold of them body and soul, and they feel the wounds and experiences of the Trial all over, in every cell of their being, they still continue to know better, to know that what is happening to them "really" doesn't exist, that it is all "figments of the mind," even when these figments are already throttling them to death. K.'s attitude to the Court, which maintains, "I am guiltless, only the great organization is guilty," is only another expression of this denial of the existence of the Court, and of the Trans in general. He feels the concrete reality of the Trial, of the Court, and of the Trans, yet his attitude is really only a constantly renewed attempt not to take these things "seriously," not to regard them as "important." This total failure to recognize the facts of the situation and the realities of the power structure is ultimately based on an attitude that regards the Trans as unreal. K. alone is really "there"—and that means his ego. What constitutes the modernity of the accused is their failure to comprehend, even during the Trial itself, that the real reality by which they are encompassed is the Trial. They endure this fact, of course—it is their destiny—but they never fight their way through to an awareness of what is actually happening, as Job did, for example, in his great Trial, which culminated, like that of Faust, in an "acquittal."

If we now return to the conversation between K. and the chaplain, we must stress once again the radical significance of the words, "Your guilt is supposed, for the present at least, to have been proved." The whole anti-fatalistic opportunity, which is man's freedom to prove his innocence, is implicit in this simple phrase, "for the present at least." Even now, at the eleventh hour, K. is given a hint of this possibility. But the attitude towards the Court that he insists on maintaining, in spite of all attempts to persuade him to the contrary, remains invincible. The self-righteousness, which always knows better, better than the Court, better even than his own inner consciousness of the Trial, plunges K. back into guilt again.

And once again K. is told that he "casts about too much for outside help, especially from women." Once again, now at the end of the story, we hear the motif which was first expressed by the Inspector at the beginning, when K. was arrested, and which might serve as a motto for all K.'s efforts at defense: "Think less about us and of what is going to happen to you, think more about yourself instead."

When K. reacts to the chaplain's emphatic warning, "Don't you see that it isn't the right kind of help?" with nothing but his usual talk about his plans and about the salaciousness of the officials, without "really" having listened, and so persists in his basic fault of not listening, exactly as he did when he was first arrested, then, at last, the chaplain's attitude changes. Even he despairs, and he shrieks, "Can't you see anything at all?" "It was an angry cry, but at the same time sounded like the involuntary shriek of one who sees another fall and is startled

out of himself." Now for the first time the priest suc-
cumbs to a mood of resignation; the Cathedral itself
seems to be affected by this atmosphere. Even the man
whose profession calls him to take up the battle against
fatalism has to recognize that in this particular case, with
this particular person, it is no longer possible to expect a
transformation. In spite of this, he is still eager to help
K.; the story entitled "Before the Law" and the whole
discussion that arose out of this story is a final attempt of
this kind.

What sort of help would still be possible, even now?
Is there, in fact, any possibility of hope and salvation for
an accused man who incurs guilt during the Trial? Yes,
there is—he can make a "confession." The moment an
accused man makes a confession, that is to say, admits
his guilt, the whole Trial inevitably takes on a new
aspect, since one of the most important functions of the
Trial, which is to induce or rather actually to compel,
the accused man to realize his guilt, has become illusory.
The whole defensive position that he has erected against
the Court has been dismantled at a stroke by the act of
confession; his perilous endopsychic erosion by the development of the Trial within himself is at an end; the
lowest stage of the process has finally been overcome.
"Until you do that"—so Leni tells K.—"there's no possibility of getting out of their clutches, none at all." The
Trial is not terminated by a confession, but it has reached
a new level. It has been extended, and moreover the
peril of a sudden execution has been eliminated; extenu-
ating circumstances can be taken into account, since an

accused man who admits his guilt already belongs to a higher order of human being than the man whose guilt is blind.

Yet even the possibility of confession is barred to K., as the chaplain probably realizes now, since "insight," i.e., "sight directed within," is one of the preconditions for any valid confession. Part of K.'s guilt arises out of his lack of relationship to his fellow human beings, and the symbol of this shortcoming is "not listening," the blatant incapacity to disregard himself even to the extent of listening to what another human being says and taking in what he means. It is precisely this unrelatedness that entangles K. over and over again in the inevitability of the Trial.

This not listening is K.'s real guilt, it is a state of being cut off both within and without; the two aspects belong together. K.'s refusal to look within, to look his feeling of guilt in the face, corresponds to his refusal to look his fellow human beings in the eyes, to recognize them in fact as human. The Court is both within and without; K. cuts himself off from both these aspects. "Confession" is not a process of "dragging one's way to the Cross"; it is an "insight," a process of making oneself conscious. If the Court requires confession, it is only requiring the recognition of what is actual, the recognition in the first place of one's own feeling of guilt. But, this recognition also means very much more. Beyond all "implied" admissions, confession involves an affirmation of the institution of the Court both in human nature and in the world. In confession we perceive and affirm the all-embracing actuality of the Trans, which is greater than man, even though it has established its seat and its basis in man. This process of making oneself conscious is confession; it recognizes the abnormality of an attitude to life and existence restricted to the narrow horizon of the ego; it is the "Sixth Hour" of Kafka's *In the Penal Colony*, i.e., the experience of the meaning of the Trial.

We have seen that the instinct which lay behind K.'s action in dismissing the Advocate was a sound one. So, too, he had often thought of the possibility, not of "some influential manipulation of the case, but of a circumvention of it, a getting rid of it altogether, a mode of living completely outside the jurisdiction of the Court." In spite of this new and correct way of formulating the question, to which there could be only one answer—confession—K. persists in his attitude of defiance. Just as he misunderstands the Court negatively as "malicious," so too he misunderstands the friendly spirit that characterizes the proceedings. Both interpretations are false and the chaplain has both of them in mind when he tells K., "You are deluding yourself about the Court."

And now follows the centerpiece of this chapter and one of the centerpieces of the whole novel—the story entitled, "Before the Law." This tells how a man from the country comes to the entrance to the Law, which is guarded by a doorkeeper, and waits there for the whole of his life, until finally he dies. The connection between this story and K.'s situation in the Cathedral is particularly significant. "In the writings which preface the Law, that particular delusion is described thus. . . ." These words are used by the chaplain to introduce the story. What is the delusion referred to here?

It is K.'s delusion about the Court and about the friendliness of the chaplain. From the story K. concludes, "So the doorkeeper deluded the man." To this the priest replies enigmatically, "Don't be too hasty, don't take over an opinion without testing it."

What is this opinion about a delusion that K. is said to have taken over? It could be the opinion of the doorkeeper, or alternatively that of the chaplain. However, when the chaplain says, "I have told you the story in the very words of the scriptures. There's no mention of delusion in it," this must mean that we have no evidence about the opinion of the doorkeeper. The chaplain must be referring to his own opinion, which K. shouldn't take over without testing. But this "opinion" of the chaplain's actually mentioned a "delusion" and it is to this that K. too is referring.

K.'s mistake is extremely revealing. The discussion of the section in "the writings" that deals with "Before the Law" is what enables us to understand it. It is typical of K. that, at once and without reflection, he chooses the passive interpretation of delusion as "being deluded by," whereas the whole point of the original story is that it demands the opposite interpretation, i.e., "deluding yourself."

The ambiguity of this single word throws a brilliant and uncanny light on the entire Trial and the way in which it is misunderstood by K. K.'s eternal, fundamental, fatal mistake is that he suffers the Trial passively instead of "conducting" it. Everything else falls into position around this basic fact. The man from the country also makes this mistake. "When he sits down on the stool by the side of the door . . . he does it of his own free will; in the story there is no mention of any compulsion." He waits for permission and forgets about his own potential for activity and his own freedom, and this forgetfulness is what leads him astray and involves him in a double misunderstanding of the doorkeeper. In the first place, the man from the country believes in the power of the doorkeeper, which is a negative overestimation of him, and on the other hand he believes in his friendliness, which is a basic overestimation of him on the positive side. Both of these mistakes arise out of a false appraisal of himself, both divert him from the right way via a roundabout way to the wrong way; they bring him to the point of begging even the fleas in the doorkeeper's fur collar for help in a task in which nobody can help him, least of all the doorkeeper, while the true help is so much closer to hand, namely in the man from the country himself. He, too, should have thought more about himself and not so much about the officials. K.'s false fixation on the Defense, on women, on help from other people—all these things are fleas in the doorkeeper's fur collar.

K.'s words, "So, the doorkeeper deluded the man," amount to a grave allegation against the whole system of the organization and its staff. The system has "gaps"; explicit mention is made of weaknesses in the character of the guard at the entrance. These gaps are due to the fact that, in addition to their capacity as representatives of the Court, the officials are also private persons, and as such are at the same time compassionate and unjust. This is a temptation to creep through the gaps in the

Law and to seek salvation by exerting influence, etc.—
but that again is the wrong way. Can it not be said,
then, that the system itself is calculated to delude the
accused? Oughtn't the doorkeeper to be thrown out of
his office at once for giving false information?

The chaplain's reply, that the doorkeeper had only
done his duty and that he was only a quite subordinate
official, implies that it is not a question of the malignity
of an individual. The doorkeeper, and in fact the officials in general, are there to do their duty, not to answer
questions. They are not even qualified to answer questions, since the information they supply, though given
in good faith, is false and delusory. The final answer is
given in the words of the chaplain: "It is not necessary
to accept everything as true, one must only accept it as
necessary."

The system with its successive stages of appeal and
the secrecy of its proceedings results in an "ignorance"
on the part of the officials which is deliberately planned
and which is only dangerous to the accused if he bothers
about other people's opinions and asks the officials. The
"ignorance" of the officials and its consequences are part
of the essential nature of the Trial procedure and of the
Court itself, which has its seat not somewhere "outside"
the accused but within him. For this very reason no one
who is involved in a Trial can be helped from "outside."
That is one of the basic premises of the nature of the
Trial; in one passage we are actually told that "the
whole onus of the Defense must be laid upon the accused himself." The whole world is built up on this principle; it is in fact part of the judicial constitution of the

world. The Court is everywhere, its officials are everywhere, but its work is split up into tiny departments and it is this that results in the ignorance of the officials. The Court has its officials everywhere, every human being is an official of the Court, everyone intervenes, even without being aware of the fact, in the Trial of his neighbor; yet everyone is "incompetent" when it comes to the "individual case."

If we say that a human being who is involved in a Trial sees the Law everywhere and that the whole world reveals itself to him as a Court with which every human being is connected, then this has the same meaning as the more objective formulation which tells us that the Court has its officials everywhere, who carry out their duties without possessing either knowledge or "competence." The accused is arrested; this means that he drinks in the Court from the whole range of being, everything has reference to him and to his Trial, and insofar as it has reference, it belongs to the Court. As we have said before, the Court observes his whole life.

An official is anyone by means of whom the Court enters into relationship with the accused, anyone who belongs to the service of the Court. But it is part of the mysterious superiority of the Trans that it can enter into relationship with the accused by way of a human being without this "official" having the slightest notion that he is in fact an official. When the Court speaks to K. out of the attitude of his Manager, even he is an "official" who belongs to the service of the Court; however, the Manager knows nothing about this and it would be absurd to ask him for information about it.

The ability of the Trans to speak through a human being is based on the transpersonality of the person concerned. The Trans can only speak through him because it has its seat in him. The other possibility, ignorance, belongs to the "private freedom" of a human being, to the purely personal part of his nature. It is for this reason that the question whether the officials do or do not delude the accused is answered by the chaplain's statement, "It is not necessary to accept everything as true, one must only accept it as necessary." The essential basis in reality for the phenomenon of "delusion," which does not entail an intention to delude others, though it certainly implies a possibility of deluding oneself, is to be found in the great split that divides the world, the officials of the Court, and humanity at large. So long as the accused clings to the "private freedom" of the officials, to their friendliness and their compassion, he deludes himself and is deluded, since it is precisely in this area that they are "incompetent" and ignorant. As officials, however, they are "transpersonal" and they are "set beyond human judgment." So the chaplain, referring to the doorkeeper, says, "Whatever he may seem to us, he is yet a servant of the Law, that is, he belongs to the Law and as such is beyond human judgment."

The officials are not the Court, but the Court stands behind them and they belong to it. It would be ridiculous, for example, if K. were to consider his Manager personally responsible for the message conveyed by way of his attitude or his words. This attempt to make the "private" part of the psyche responsible for the message spoken in it or through it by the transpersonal part is precisely what constitutes the delusion. We can only ask for information from private persons (which is the wrong way) or from the transpersonal element in ourselves (which is the right way). K., like the man from the country, invariably chooses the first alternative, never the second.

However, once we become aware of the transpersonality of the officials, a whole section of the conversation between K. and the chaplain—the discussion of the opinion that the doorkeeper is really the one who is deluded —will appear in a very puzzling light.

The assertion is there made that the doorkeeper himself is afraid of the interior of the Law, which he holds up as a bogey to the man from the country; in contrast to the man, he has no desire to enter into the Law, he is not acquainted with its interior, or at any rate he has never penetrated its depths, and he is exactly as deluded about the "aspect and significance of the interior" as the man from the country himself. The doorkeeper is only there for the sake of this man and he is actually subordinate to him even in knowledge, for the man sees the radiance that streams from the entrance to the Law, which the doorkeeper cannot see.

On the whole the story entitled "Before the Law" confirms the insights that have already emerged in the course of the Trial; however, the section we are considering now does play a unique part. Although its basic contents can be reconciled with the results we have reached so far, they are not confirmed by the rest of the text.

What we have here is a speculation that no longer re-

lates to K.'s individual Trial but to the institution of the
Trial procedure as such; it dares, if we may say so, to
approach the Trans itself.

The Court by no means prohibits criticism of the proceedings; in fact, the arrangements of the Trial make it
inevitable that the Court and the various ways in which
it impinges on life only manifest themselves to the accused in visible form in the course of his own Trial. The
very existence of the Court may be disputed by the accused—let alone the binding validity of its judgments—
but it is part of the unique nature of this Court that it
integrates all kinds of behavior towards itself into the
actual conduct of the proceedings. The Court is that
which is absolutely superior, and no mortal can evade its
supreme authority. It is possible to dispute the existence
of a deep region and of a Trans—K. is not the only person who does that—but the deep layer continues to op-
erate in spite of the various points of view that can be
adopted towards it. These points of view—the attitudes
of belief and disbelief, of knowing and willing—are all
filed among the "records" of the Court, which means
that they also help to determine the mode of operation
of the deep layer. The question whether a man is conscious or unconscious of the Court is of crucial importance, since it largely determines the way in which the
Court will conduct itself towards him. But even these
modes of reaction of the Court are part of the Law,
whereas the points of view which can be adopted towards
it are no more than "opinions," and we are told that "the
scriptures are unalterable and the comments often

enough merely express the commentators' bewilderment."

"The scriptures" or "the Law" represent that which is given prior to everything else; it is there before everything and it embraces everything. The scriptures are the embodiment of the Trans, which dominates everything that happens. Apart from the Trans, the Law is the only thing that "really" exists, it is that which is "indubitable," that which the man who sees through "reality" does not discuss, but accepts as the starting point.

Yet does not this involve a strange and really absurd dogmatism? Is it adequate to argue, "He belongs to the Law and as such is set beyond human judgment"? Is it possible for us to understand at all the certainty that lies behind such a statement as "It is the Law that has placed him at his post; to doubt his integrity is to doubt the Law itself"?

The answer to this question is the "Trial" itself. The Trial happens to a human being who would have answered this question unhesitatingly in the negative and who would certainly have replied to the statement, "To doubt his integrity is to doubt the Law itself," by saying, "So what?" as most of us would have done. What is really so disturbing about the Trial is that each of us experiences it in his own person because he identifies himself with Joseph K. and would in fact behave as he does. (It is for this reason that the Trial is for the most part so profoundly misunderstood.)

The Trial demonstrates that the Court is a reality about which many opinions may be held—yet it is a reality, too, that everyone has to reckon with, since it is nothing less than the Law of the world. The world is built on the pattern of this Law, and everyone who lives in it is subject to its jurisdiction.

The power that created this legal constitution of the world and is forever creating it anew is carried by man in himself. The accused is not delivered up as a passive victim to this Court as if it were an external secular tribunal. The Trial takes place in and through the accused himself—as well, of course, as "on" himself. The accused belongs to the Court just as much as the officials do, and if it is true as we observed elsewhere that K., the accused man, directs his own Trial, so that the Court as it were is in his service, we can now formulate this position by saying that the deep layer in him, the Trans, which is the source of all these happenings, is the same as that dimension which, in the case of the officials, we termed their transpersonality. In the officials, this transpersonal element operates independently of their ignorance and incompetence; in K.'s Trial, however, it gains the upper hand against the resistance of K.'s private ego-consciousness, which moans, argues, and denies. The only difference is that the officials are passively pervious to the irradiating influence of the transpersonal, whereas K. has a Trial, that is to say a confrontation, in which the private personal part of his nature is gripped by his transpersonality, the deep layer in him, the Trans, and compelled to recognize and to become conscious of the Trans.

We are now better placed to suggest a solution for our initial problem, the position of the doorkeeper. The chaplain tells us that without knowing it the doorkeeper is "subordinated to" the man from the country, since he has to wait until the man deigns to come to the door of the Law at which the doorkeeper performs his service.

As we have seen, the Trial originated in K. himself, his guilt "called" for it; everything else was only a consequence of this guilt. This "calling" of the guilt that is the starting point of the Trial does not proceed from the Trans alone, since the Court reacts solely to this call. It is true that K.'s speedy acceptance of the arrest presupposes a certain erosion of his conscious mind and of its rigid conscious attitude, yet on the other hand the Trial itself as it unfolds before us proves just how difficult it is to disturb this same conscious attitude of "innocence." What, then, is the meaning of this calling, if the caller is neither the Trans nor K.'s conscious mind?

It is just because K.'s conscious mind is so far removed from the Trans that the wound of isolation "calls," and it actually signals in two directions. It is heard in the Trans, but it also makes itself audible in K.'s conscious mind, in his ego. But whereas the Trans reacts immediately, by sending out the warders, K.'s conscious mind avoids acknowledging the call, though he has heard it distinctly enough.

The call of the guilt is the first stage. It is only then that the intervention of the Court follows; only then that man enters the sphere of justice. Once he is arrested, man stands "at the door of the Law."

There is one basic difference that distinguishes K. and the man from the country from the officials: the direction in which they face. All the officials have their backs to the

law, in every sense of that term. K. faces it. The officials
are bound to the place in which they render their service.
K. is free; his Trial gives him the opportunity of ac-
quainting himself with the entire territory of the Court,
including its interior. The inner development of the
Trial is essentially a process in which K. or at least a
part of K. executes the Trial on his own person and
progressively, as the Trial unfolds, gains an insight into
his own guilt. If K. could bring himself to the point of
confession, something tremendous would happen to
him: the Court, the interior of the Law, would reveal
itself to him. He would have experienced and would
"know" the reality of the Law, its significance in the
constitution of the world, and its infinite superiority.
Through the events of his own individual Trial, he
would have recognized and experienced the community
of being between his own essential self, his nature as a
transpersonality, and the Trans of the Law, and as a
result he would have achieved an approach to the Trans
that would have raised him to quite another plane of
existence, far beyond guilt and judgment.

It is now clear in what respect the man from the country is superior to the doorkeeper. He desires to enter into
the Law; something within him constrains him to do
so. He is exposing himself to something of which the
doorkeeper and the officials are afraid, namely to the
logical conclusion of the Trial. Every official instinctively suspects the torment that must be involved in this
process, yet his partial viewpoint prevents him from sur-
veying the total significance of the happening. At the
end of his Trial the accused—both with and against his

own consent—is overtaken and conquered by Justice. At the same time, however, even if he has not made a confession, he does perceive a part of the whole; he sees the radiance that streams from the entrance to the Law. If K.'s struggle is the unavailing struggle of K., the private person, against the Court and against the transpersonality within himself, then this transpersonality sees things more and more searchingly and compels the other K. to accept a deeper and deeper insight.

Every charge therefore clearly represents an opportunity; it confronts the accused with the central task of entering into the Law. The basic shortcoming of K. and of the man from the country, which inveigles them into concealing this opportunity from themselves, is their passivity, the denial of their own transpersonality. Despite his knowledge of his participation in the events of his Trial, which can in fact only take place if he recognizes it, and despite his growing insight into his guilt, K. never succeeds in identifying himself with the active, transpersonal part of his nature. Always, however vainly, he struggles against it, or (if his strength fails him), he simply lets himself drop. His conscious mind, his ego, remains accusing, suffering, and "raped." His active energy remains stranded on the outskirts, caught by the "fleas in the doorkeeper's fur collar."

At this point, however, we are faced by a general question. Who is the accused man and whose guilt is it that calls out for the Law?

There is a possibility that any human being may be accused, since "the door leading into the law stands open as usual," and the man from the country even asserts that "Everyone strives to attain the Law." Yet it is distinctly stated that not every human being is brought to Trial. Does this mean that people who have a Trial are particularly bad, and that the others are guiltless? There is no doubt that all human beings are guilty, because they offend the World Law of Justice. However, only a small fraction of them have an original, though often buried, awareness of this fact. It is these people who have a refined consciousness of guilt, a superior instinct for justice, that are put on Trial. It is from them that the cry for the Court arises. That is the explanation of the paradoxical statement that for the initiated the group of the accused is immediately recognizable, since they are distinguished from other people by their "attractiveness."

It does seem at times as if the warders come "of their own accord," as if the intrusion of the Trans into the life of a human being happens "spontaneously," but as the events of the Trial revolve in their sequence, it can be shown, invariably and without exception, that the person concerned participates in this initiative. What we have here is an example of the important truth that the Trans is in a certain sense "passive"; this, too, is probably an essential part of the constitution of Justice in the world.

There is, however, one qualifier to this statement. Any kind of happening may provide an occasion for the intrusion of the Trans into the life of a human being. Any kind of experience can trigger a sudden change in which the life of a human being may be transformed. The occasion can be a tree, a landscape, a "knock at the yard-door," a "neighbor"—anything in the world, in fact, since "everything belongs to the Court." The occasion may also be a voluntary, fully conscious attempt by one human being to bring about this change in the life of another. An "occasion" of this kind differs from other possible causes inasmuch as the person who brings it about is acting consciously. This means that he is conscious of the transpersonality in himself and is a "knowing" official, and we could therefore say, as for example in the case of the chaplain, that the Trans had taken the initiative in his person. Yet even here, the arrested man is always the true "realizer" of the events of the Trial. In the final analysis, the person who calls him is only a "cause" or "initiator" of what happens in the Trial.

The constitution of the world and of the Court finds its place of fulfillment only in man; it is through him that Justice comes into existence, through his knowledge of Justice that Justice is done. Once we have grasped this fact, the ambiguous and grotesque physiognomy of the Trial reveals its true character. The ambiguity and uncanniness are in fact to be found in the person of the accused. His ignorance and his half-knowledge are reflected in the kind of happening that occurs in the Trial. The more knowledge a man has, the clearer it becomes to him that the world, the events of the Trial, and the Trans all partake of the character of Justice—and vice versa.

In modern times, however, we are confronted by human beings for whom life disconnected from the Trans, life lived from the head alone, is the reality of their daily experience. It is those human beings who intuitively suspect that they are disconnected in this way and who

nourish a hidden feeling of guilt, because something—
perhaps even the one thing necessary—is missing from
their lives—human beings who are sensitive enough to
feel constricted by the limitations and narrowness of
their conscious minds, those are the people who are
brought to Trial.

At first sight this hypothesis seems nonsensical; it
seems to stand the whole Trial on its head. Yet I am
convinced that such a hypothesis is necessary. How else
are we to explain why, at the very beginning of the
Trial, K. is pursued by such an acute feeling of guilt
that he actually tells Frau Grubach, "If you want to keep
your house respectable you'll have to begin by giving me
notice." And how else are we to understand K.'s unconscious recognition of the proceedings? K.'s refined
feeling of guilt is actually identical with that obscure
knowledge of his transpersonality which we had already
identified as the motive force behind the Trial. It is only
those human beings who—over and above their "private
freedom"—are also instinctively aware of their transpersonality that possess such an exact sense of guilt as this.
The Trial is a confrontation between these two parts of
the psyche—the inner development and final victory of
the transpersonal and the Trans and the decline or
rather the collapse of the ego.

It is therefore the "attractive" people, the people who
are above the average, that undergo the inferno of the
Trial and are tormented and finally executed by the
Law. But is *that* supposed to be Justice?

Kafka's answer to this question is quite certainly
Yes. The way of the Trial, through the instrumentality

of that fateful engine of execution, the Court, is one of the few ways—and in terms of the Trial the only way—in which it is possible for a human being to approach the Trans. The Trial is man's unique opportunity to reach the Court and via the Court to arrive at the Trans and so to outsoar even the officials—rather in the spirit of the saying in the scriptures that "The sinner who repents is higher than the righteous."

If the Trial is seen as the struggle of the transpersonal for the mastery in man, it also represents, by the same token, man's birth into the transpersonal and man's way into the interior of the Law. That is why even when, as in the case of the man from the country, the Trial is unsuccessful and the man does not even pass through the door of the Law, we are finally told that he "perceives the radiance that streams . . . from the door of the Law." Even when confession does not bring insight into the nature of the Law, or when, as in *In the Penal Colony*, the Sixth Hour, which brings death, does not also bring insight and redemption, man, the accused, still approaches the radiance that is to be found in the interior of the Law.

We can now understand the doorkeeper's saying, "This door was intended only for you." Each Trial is an individual process and is conducted in an individual way; the proceedings are entirely adapted to the individuality of the accused. This is the accused's only way to the Law.

The moment in time when the Trial begins, what sparks it into flame, the particular way in which the life of the accused takes shape, how the struggle between the deep region and the ego of the accused develops, what defeats and victories, insights and illusions are experienced by him—yes, and even how far he is brought by the Trial, whether into the interior of the Law or only as far as its outermost entrance—all these things are individual, they make up the life of that particular person, they are "his" way and his destiny.

This is why the Court, the whole body of the officials, are all "his" institutions, so that we could say that they are all there simply "for" the accused. He is the master of the Court. That man should enter into the interior of the Law is nothing less than the meaning of the world. The entrance at which the doorkeeper stands is really only negotiable by this one person, and although we are told at the beginning of the Trial that the doorkeeper "cannot admit the man at the moment," later on it would have been both possible and necessary for the man to have entered through the door and actively to have conquered the territories of the Court. But this passage also enables us to give reasons for the priest's rejection of the doorkeeper's statement, "I am now going to shut it" (i.e., the door). It is no doubt true that this way to the Law, via the Trial, is only negotiable by this one person. However, it is an essential part of the constitution of the world as a whole that it is possible for human beings to arrive at the Trans by way of the Justice of the Trial. "The door leading into the Law stands open as usual," irrespective of whether an individual makes his way through it or not.

Here too the objective becomes visible in the subjective, but in spite of this it remains objective. Though the

Trial is enacted in and on the person of the individual, Justice is part of the constitution of the world and is independent of the individual, although it has its place of fulfillment in him.

The end of the Cathedral chapter demonstrates once again the futility of all attempts to help K. Foolishly, he misses the point of the entire happening. "A melancholy conclusion," he remarks to the priest. "It turns lying into a universal principle." The chaplain does not contradict him; he realizes the futility of any reply. K. is tired; he thinks that these "intangibles" are "better suited to a theme for discussion among Court officials than for him." Here, too, as always, K. is entangled in the "tangible"; he does not see that what appears to him to be "real" is actually unreal, and vice versa. In fact, if we think about this very symbol of "reality," the whole question of understanding and misunderstanding becomes clear. K.— and a whole world that shares his outlook—fails to see that "reality" is what "really" works, so that although it is perfectly possible to deny the deep region, the Trans, and Justice as the ultimate constitution of the world, this simply does not work. In reality the "intangibles" do K. to death, whereas the so-called "real" things about him—his common sense, his conscious argumentation and objections, and the way he makes fun of the "illusions" of so-called unreality—impart a spectral character to his own existence. His superstition about "reality" turns him into a phantom which does not see things that are real and sees things which are not real.

At this point K. would like to leave the Cathedral, but he is surprised and actually complains when the priest agrees to let him go. And now, once more and for the very last time, the priest formulates the real state of affairs in a way that implies the infinite superiority of the Court: "It receives you when you come and it relinquishes you when you go."

The Trans behaves passively; it has built the world in such a way that you can always come to the Trans and it is ready—always and eternally ready—to receive you. It sends out warders to arrest you if you call for arrest and it gives advice when it is asked for advice. But once you enter into its kingdom, you are unconditionally subject to the lawful jurisdiction of that kingdom, and nothing, literally nothing, can alter the slightest tittle of that law. The Trans holds nobody and needs nobody, it demands nothing and it asks no questions: it is the Law and its nature is Justice.

The last chapter, which is Chapter Ten, contains K.'s final downfall. Yet here, more clearly perhaps than ever before, we see K.'s participation in the happening, and in fact his positive domination of events.

K. is sitting there already waiting for the visit and is actually putting on gloves—as if for a funeral—when the men in frock coats come to take him away. At first his resistance flares up again. But neither his cry "Why did they send you, of all people!" nor his resolution, "I shan't need my strength much longer, I'll expend all the strength I have," contain any more real strength or conviction; they are simply ripples on the surface of his will. Very quickly his inner preparedness carries the day. When someone who seems like Fräulein Bürstner appears in front of them, "it did not matter to K. whether

it was really Fräulein Bürstner or not; the important
thing was that he suddenly realized the futility of resistance."

And now K. experiences the decisive change, the crucial insight, with a matter-of-factness and even, we
might almost say, with a gentleness that can only be explained by the length of the period during which this
change has been prepared for in the psyche. There is
nothing heroic about his resistance. He obeys the warning that had been whispered to him by the appearance
of the girl. And it is a K. who has been transformed by
the Trial that now says: "I always wanted to snatch at
the world with twenty hands, and not for a very laudable
motive either. That was wrong, and am I to show now
that not even a whole year's struggling with my case has
taught me anything? Am I to leave this world as a man
who shies away from all conclusions? Are people to say
of me after I am gone that at the beginning of my case
I wanted it to finish, and at the end of it I wanted it to
begin again? I don't want that to be said. I am grateful
for the fact that these half-dumb stupid creatures have
been sent to accompany me on this journey, and that I
have been left to say to myself all that is needed."

It is the Sixth Hour; the radiance from the door of the
Law has now reached him, and with the dignity that
illumines the beauty of the accused he brings his protest
to an end. He, who had just before been offended because more had not been made of his execution, now
recognizes the real reason why these particular men had
been sent to him and no others. It is his death and it is
he that has to come to terms with it; and it is in fact

nothing less than the respect of the Court which leaves him in this decisive hour alone with himself.

His two companions now become nothing more than pliant satellites and their subordinate status is beyond all question. And K. himself is now so far gone that he actually runs to meet his death.

Yet in spite of everything K. remains K., right up to the bitter end. As the two assistants hand the knife over him from side to side, we are told that "K. now perceived clearly that he was supposed to seize the knife himself, as it traveled from hand to hand above him, and plunge it into his own breast. But he did not do so, he merely turned his head, which was still free to move, and gazed around him. He could not completely rise to the occasion, he could not relieve the officials of all their tasks; the responsibility for this last failure of his lay with him who had not left him the remnant of strength necessary for the deed."

With a cruelly tormenting futility, the attitude of protest breaks through once again. K. knows that he is in the very act of proving his worthiness—yet he has to be right, his ego, steeped as it is in vanity, cannot hold back from the ultimate reproach: "The authorities are guilty, He is guilty." (Here for the first time, beyond the Trans of the Court, a He appears.) Why has not He given me the strength?

And now in the last second before his death, as in the vision of a man who is falling precipitately from a height, a different world-picture bursts into view—too late. He sees right behind him at the window of a house, a human figure who stretches out his arms—is it to K.?

In a flash we remember his observation on the way to the place of execution: "At one lighted tenement window some babies were playing behind bars, reaching with their little hands towards each other although not able to move themselves from the spot." And as K. sees this human figure, thoughts come tumbling into his mind: "Who was it? A friend? A good man? Someone who sympathized? Someone who wanted to help? Was it one person only? Or were they all there? Was help at hand?" And he raises his hands and spreads out all the fingers in the ultimate question of his despair: "Where was the Judge whom he had never seen? Where was the High Court, to which he had never penetrated?"

And then comes death. But that is only the process of dying, it is not the end. With failing eyes K. sees "the two of them, cheek leaning against cheek, immediately before his face, watching the final act." What is this final act, and what is there that still remains to be decided when death is already present, on the spot?

" 'Like a dog!' he said: it was as if he meant the shame of it to outlive him."

K. knows what final act this is; he knows that they are waiting for him. Even if he has not already brought about his own death, they are still waiting for his consent. And split as K.'s life had been, wilting into torment, so too was this most cruel of all deaths. It was cruel because K. himself had made it so. He does not say yes, but he says no to his own no. He reviles himself and complains in the same breath. Why is it that he can't do it? He dies like a dog. Why doesn't he reach out for the radiance that streams from the door of the Law?

Doesn't he see it? He sees it all right. But he only sees it—unsatisfied, despairing, and deviant as always—through the veil of his own shame: shame because he did not bring about his own death and because he did not say yes to the death that they gave him.

This shame will outlive him, or so he believes; and once again he does not see that this very shame is the yes that was required of him; K. does not know that the torment of this shame is the expiation and resolution for the concealment of his yes.

II

CHAGALL AND THE BIBLE

Marc Chagall's illustrated Bible, an oeuvre that took
more than twenty years to complete, has now, in Chagall's old age, emerged from seclusion and is available
for viewing by our own generation.[1] The work has both
strong points and weaknesses; plates of exceptional power are to be found in juxtaposition with graceful, agree-
able pieces and with others, though only quite rarely,
which do not seem to us to possess any remarkable significance at all; however, the consistency of the overall
design and the depth of inner feeling that is maintained
throughout embraces even these. It embraces everything
and all things: creation and destruction, vocation and
apostasy, ascent to the heights and wanderings in the
wilderness, life and death, the primal age of archaic man
and the most living, immediate present—like the Bible
itself, that unique book, which is as inexhaustible and as

"Chagall und die Bibel," *Merkur* (Stuttgart), no. 130 (Dec. 1958).

1. [Marc Chagall: *La Bible*, 105 etchings and 28 lithographs,
with a text by Jean Wahl and an appreciation by Meyer Schapiro,
constituting a double number of *Verve: Revue artistique et
littéraire* (Paris), VIII, nos. 33 and 34 (1956). Also published
with translated texts as *Illustrations for the Bible*, by Marc
Chagall (New York: Harcourt, Brace, 1956). The parenthetical
numbers in this essay refer to the plates in *Verve*.]

rich in strata of meaning as the world itself in which man exists.

Throughout history, the art of the West has been decisively influenced by this Biblical world, and a colorful stream of pictures—from the earliest miniatures right down to the illustrations of modern times and from the altarpieces of churches and the wall paintings in great houses to the museums of the present day—has fertilized the life of the West.

But what an astonishing Biblical world this is, a world in which medieval footsoldiers under the command of Joshua march around a Jericho somewhere in central Germany, while Moses, beautifully robed and devoutly praying, looks on as armies of knights contend in battle! It is a world, this, of magnificent kings, of prophets in would-be classical attire, looking half like Hellenistic philosophers and half like old men with long beards carrying symbolical volumes, of beautiful Greek Josephs and Davids, of Renaissance nudes disguised and disrobed as Bathsheba or Susannah—of images significant and splendid, insignificant and trivial—of a sea of figures. And then, in the middle of this sea, the dark and alien island of the people which, dispersed among the nations that paint and carve, has itself remained without images, yet whose life is filled to its bitter, bitter brim with the reality of this book, the people, moreover, which in its secret presence, despised by all, exists as the living continuation of this book. For the Christian West, all this was archaic prehistory, which had taken place long ago in the Middle East, holy and edifying stories or prophetic allegories, such as the sacrifice of Isaac or the youthful Joseph in the well, King David or the Suffering Servant of the

Lord. It is for this people alone that these stories represent the history of their own ancestors and the living reality which—whether the individual knows it or not—finds its present expression in his own inner history.

The figure of the Synagogue, which is pilloried in the cathedrals, with the broken scepter of her sovereignty and the bandage veiling her eyes, is actually a true symbol of this people. Robbed of its share in the natural world and of the organization of that world by man, it was compelled to live exclusively in the world of the Bible, viewed with the vision of the inner eye. And it did in fact live in fidelity to that world, not only by keeping the Law and elaborating the interior world-systems of its mystical philosophy, which is rooted in the images, words, and letters of this book, but by bearing perennial witness, in its living and in its dying, which have endured for hundreds and thousands of years, to the indissoluble connection which binds it to this book.

It is no accident that today, when the reality of the old Synagogue has come to an end and the Jewish people is emerging from its *insular* condition and opening its eyes anew, that for the first time a painter belonging to this people should attempt the task of representing the Bible as his own world, as the inner world of Jewish reality. At this point, there shine out upon us, close at hand and unapproachable at the same time, the paintings of Rembrandt, the only Western artist in whose work the inner world of the Bible has been given—so very frequently—an adequate embodiment. That Chagall's achievement in this field is not obliterated by the very thought of Rembrandt is surprising enough. What is even more surprising, however, is the fact that in our present epoch of disintegration a man should be found who possesses the power to enter legitimately into the spirit of this world and to represent it in terms of his own art.

That it was possible for these illustrations of the Bible to be created during the decades of the European holocaust can only be understood as an expression of that Jewish faith which cannot be annihilated by any historical disaster and which holds fast to the eternal covenant of God with man and to the reliance placed by Jewish man on that covenant. The very fact that there is no longer any external religious bond that holds modern man (whether Jewish or Western) makes the breakthrough to faith of the isolated, lonely individual, such as Rembrandt, or in this case Chagall, an achievement of general moral validity and a true expression of our time. Admittedly, this breakthrough to faith does not bring with it any security; what it does do, however, is to reveal the indissoluble bond of relationship linking man with the godhead who remains hidden in darkness, and whose "present absence" has to be endured as a self-evident fact of life. This "remaining-in-darkness" is one of the few features in which Chagall's work becomes almost heretical; the more human world of the Bible, in which the presence of God is so open and obvious, changes imperceptibly and is modernized. The world of the angel now occupies the foreground, while the godhead itself appears almost always abstractly, in the monogram of the Divine Name, which is inscribed within the gloriole.

How familiar Western art has made us with stories of the Creation, which take the form of God creating the plants, the animals, and man in an immense number of paradises, all deluged in color! The white-bearded old men who reached their culmination in Michelangelo's flying Wind-Spirit figure of God have left a definite mark on the patriarchal God-image of the West. Characteristically, Chagall has omitted practically the whole story of the Creation from his black-and-white illustrations of the Bible. For him, the creative activity of God has withdrawn into the imageless anonymity of the numinous that is typical of the later Jewish conception of the godhead.

In fact, the first plate in Chagall's Bible has a curiously Gnosticizing effect and is almost unique, since it flatly contradicts the text it illustrates. (The other "deviation," too, the replacement of the angel by the gloriole of the Divine Name in the Call of Moses at the Burning Bush [27] points in the same direction.) In the almost entirely black space of the pre-Creation void, a tall, bearded, and robed angel is gliding downwards; above him is the ball of light inscribed with the Name of God, from which a stream of light pours down upon everything in this picture that is brightly illumined. His face, which the light reveals in profile, is turned backwards. Where, into what past or future, is this extraordinary angel gazing, as he hastens down to earth with his burden? On his arm he is carrying the naked, sleeping body of Adam, white-gleaming and ungainly; and here, too, we have to ask ourselves a question. "Is he really carrying this form, or is he not rather himself this form of Adam, which is in his own image, and which appears to be as it were grown together with his own form to such an extent that the arm of the angel who is carrying him and the arm of the sleeping Adam are actually identical?" No God creates this Adam out of a clod of earth, no breath of God is breathed into him, but in his childlike spiritual-bodily form, out of the white light of the godhead to which he belongs, he is borne down sleeping into the world of earth.

At this point, we are confronted with a very strange contrast. In the whole of Chagall's illustrations of the Bible, the bodily form of man, with all its ungainly, musty earthiness, is never really overcome. It is as if this figure, in its unlovely clumsiness, only fully comes to life when it is animated by the breath of the Spirit of the godhead. It is not one single breath of the Divine Spirit that makes him, once and for all, a living soul, but his formlessness has to be given form over and over, his un-createdness created ever anew, by the moving Spirit-breath that breathes upon him or by the Spirit-storm of the living godhead that uproots him. But here, at the beginning, in the first plate on the Creation, a gleaming spirit-body sleeps on the arm of the angel who has grown into oneness with him and is borne down through the darkness to the "dark earth."[2]

There is an almost unbearable and yet entirely necessary antithesis between the first and the last plate in Chagall's Bible. The last plate is an illustration of the verses that describe the call of Ezekiel.

> . . . Open thy mouth, and eat that I give thee. And when I looked, behold, an hand was sent unto me; and, lo, a roll of a book was therein; And he spread it before

2. ["dunklen Erde," quoted from Goethe's poem "Selige Sehnsucht" ("Hallowed Yearning"), in his *West-Eastern Divan.*—Tr.]

me: and it was written within and without: and there was written therein lamentations, and mourning, and woe. . . . And he said unto me, Son of man, cause thy belly to eat, and fill thy bowels with this roll that I give thee. Then did I eat it; and it was in my mouth as honey for sweetness. [Ezek. 2:8-10, 3:3, AV]

The demand made by this divine mission, which could serve as a motto for the whole series of Chagall's illustrations of the Bible, is so overwhelming that on this last etching no trace of the sweetness of honey is to be found. It is as though it had vanished into thin air, somewhere along the mighty orbit described by the 105 plates in their sequence. All we can see of the prophet is his shoulder-girdle, tightly pressed against the bottom of the plate, his arms raised aloft and his face gazing upwards. But practically the whole surface of the picture is taken up by the scroll, which is portrayed as shining in a stream of light and held by a gigantic arm that stretches down from a dark cloud. The bearded head of the prophet—is it the head of a Christ or of a rabbi?—with its left eye open and its right eye closed and its tender, sensitive half-opened mouth, is expressive of sheer acceptance and suffering, the helplessly willing acceptance of an overpowering mission that cannot possibly be accomplished. And in fact, how could the prophet possibly eat and digest this gigantic object, written within and without, this scroll, which is unrolling itself before him, when its dimensions so incomparably exceed the capacity of this mouth, this head, this human being, to take it in? Again and again, in a new form every time, we encounter this same conflict. A being who is human-only-human is exposed and delivered up to the almost unfulfillable demands of the living suprahuman power within himself which he experiences as a mission from the godhead.

And the eyes. These are not the only eyes whose significance in Chagall's illustrations of the Bible arises specifically from the fact that they seem to stand right out from the context of the work as a whole. An example is the angel at the sacrifice of Isaac (10) [cf. fig. 1], one of the most powerful images in the entire series. The figure of Abraham is a dark mass, crouching over the body of Isaac, his son, which is stretched out, a white victim, prepared for the sacrifice. The huge knife, near the point of which the delicate toy ram of the real victim can be seen, stands up tall and rigid in Abraham's fist, which is raised towards heaven. Only a part of Abraham's face, set stiffly in the obedience of despair, and only a tiny piece of his eye, looking upwards in hesitant expectation, is in the light. An angel shoots down like a dive bomber, light upon light, thrusting his way through the stormy darkness of the father, who is almost lost in the night. But the eye of this angel—which is the only part visible (the other eye is on the dark side of his face, which is, as it were, cut off from the light)—sees neither Abraham nor the victim made ready for the sacrifice, neither the earth nor anything earthly at all, but is sheer mission, the divine message made incarnate. No angelic arm, in humanly-suprahuman fashion, grasps the humanly-inhuman arm of the sacrificial father. A missile of light pierces the darkness—nothing else. No trace of an encounter, of I and Thou, of a vis-à-vis. Nothing but message and command, and now the withdrawal of the command by a light, radiating from the light, from the king of kings.

The angel's eye never leaves the charmed circle of the
influence of the godhead, it never sees anything other
than the godhead, it never sees the human realm, even
when it is carrying out missions and delivering messages
in the terrestrial sphere. Even the mighty angels who
bring a call from God (91 and 100) do not see those
whom they are calling—they do not even see Isaiah and
Jeremiah. Even the angels leave man in a solitude unmitigated by any proximity of the divine. It seems as if
man is only seen when he himself sees the unseen. It is
not until then that he achieves the reality which is peculiarly his own. And there is in fact a certain closeness
and kinship between man and the angels in this very
circumstance, since man too, like the angels, only lives
insofar as he is open to the divine; it is only when the
spirit-body of Adam which lives in every man begins to
glow that man's capacity to be the image of God, to be
in fact a form without form, is finally realized. It is then
that the creative afflatus of the godhead makes the clumsiness of the corporeal into a living soul. That is why the
people of Chagall's Biblical world are not "stamped
patterns" and—unlike the tremendous, superhuman
figures of Michelangelo—are certainly not "beautiful
forms."

The people of the earliest times from Noah and Abraham to Moses and Joseph, the judges and kings in the
world of the so-called historical period, and the prophets
shaken by the tempest of the godhead—on every plate
these figures exhibit a new and different countenance.
Perhaps the most striking evidence of the scope of man's
capacity for transformation is provided by the man wear-
ing the crown—the king. Saul, David, Solomon, Pharaoh

—the simple juxtaposition of these names enables us to comprehend the gulf that yawns between the eternal, statue-like God-King of Egypt and the open and exposed existence of the kings of the Old Testament. That is why the Pharaoh of the Exodus with the "hardened heart" looks like a doll (29 and 30) which falls over when pushed by anything alive, for its wooden immobility is the immobility of a toy king. It is only when man is not king from all eternity, when this kingship is given to him by God and can be taken away from him again, that he enters upon the destiny whose drama is played out between the divine and the human dimensions; it is this alone of which the Bible speaks.

Strangely enough, however, this exceedingly individual approach does not preclude the simultaneous disclosure within it of something typical and even archetypal. A character in the Bible may be portrayed as a young man: for example, we see the young Joseph, the young David, the young Solomon. Yet how different they are in the way their youth expresses itself, and at the same time how much they have in common with each other! We see Joseph in the primitive beauty of a natural sense of having been "chosen" (18); it is only after he has been cast into the pit (19) that he achieves a new and quite different kind of childlikeness when, rapt in concentration as he interprets Pharaoh's dreams, and now looking almost ugly, he does not see Pharaoh standing before him but the world of Pharaoh's dreams and of his own mission (22). And then there is the boy David in the arms of Samuel, who is anointing him as king; David is almost maidenly in his utter openness to the happening that is transforming him (60). How different on the other hand is the young Solomon, portrayed as the king who in his dream prays to God for wisdom (77). How much more individual and less archetypal he is than Joseph or David—yet it was he who in his maturity became the fairy-tale king of wisdom (80 and 81). The figure of Solomon as represented by Chagall reaches out to other and later times than those of the Bible; his meeting with the Queen of Sheba (80) and his almost baroque appearance on the lion throne (81) are charged with the magic fragrance of the fairy-tale world of the Arabian Nights and the Jewish Haggada. These stories bear eloquent witness to the wonderful unity of a memory which spans earlier and later ages.

David, too, when he is portrayed as the anointed boy (60), as the slayer of Goliath (63), as the father mourning for his son (73), and as the man enraptured by God (76) is derived from different "ages" and from different spheres of reality. Then there is Jacob wrestling with the angel in all the strength of his virility (16), Jacob the uncannily cowering figure to whom they have just brought Joseph's bloodstained coat (20), a rock of pain, primeval and almost beyond humanity in his despair, surmounted in a semicircle by the fools' heads of his gesticulating sons, and then the enchanting plate of Jacob's homecoming to Joseph, the son who has been found again and who has been raised to high office in Egypt (24) [cf. fig. 2]. The way he sits there on the back of the camel, the Old Man, beaming like a child, overwhelmed by the tenderness of his rapture in the godhead, because everything is all right again, everything has been guided into the right paths with such a magisterial hand! He is riding in the light, entirely outside and above the milling crowd of men, children, and animals. All of them belong to him, they are traveling with him, yet he in his joy is not with them but with his beloved son, who was lost and has now been given back to him. He is riding in the halo of his wisdom; he is the father of them all, the Old, Old Man, and at the same time he is like a little tiny child in his gratitude to his God for the miracle of this divine surprise. And then, on the next plate (25), the blessing of Ephraim and Manasseh, we see the same Jacob, as a rock of immemorial light. He gazes into the future as though through the great window opposite which he is sitting. He blesses the boys, and the radiant power which pours out from him is so great that those he has blessed seem to hide their heads under his hands, and even Joseph is dazzled and holds one hand in front of his eyes, while with the other hand he covers his throbbing heart, because the strength of the aged patriarch overpowers him, young as he is.

And Joseph was not just one of the sons, not just someone who had been cast into a pit and raised to high office in Egypt, but a man who from his youth up had lived with dreams of the godhead, and now in his maturity was preparing the future destiny of his family and of a whole people. The same eyes which at this moment cannot endure the glory of his father were open in childlike innocence in his vision before Pharaoh and are filled with an almost superhuman knowledge when he makes himself known to his brethren, and Benjamin, the beloved youngest brother, sinks down upon Joseph's breast (23). The group of the two brothers corresponds—as

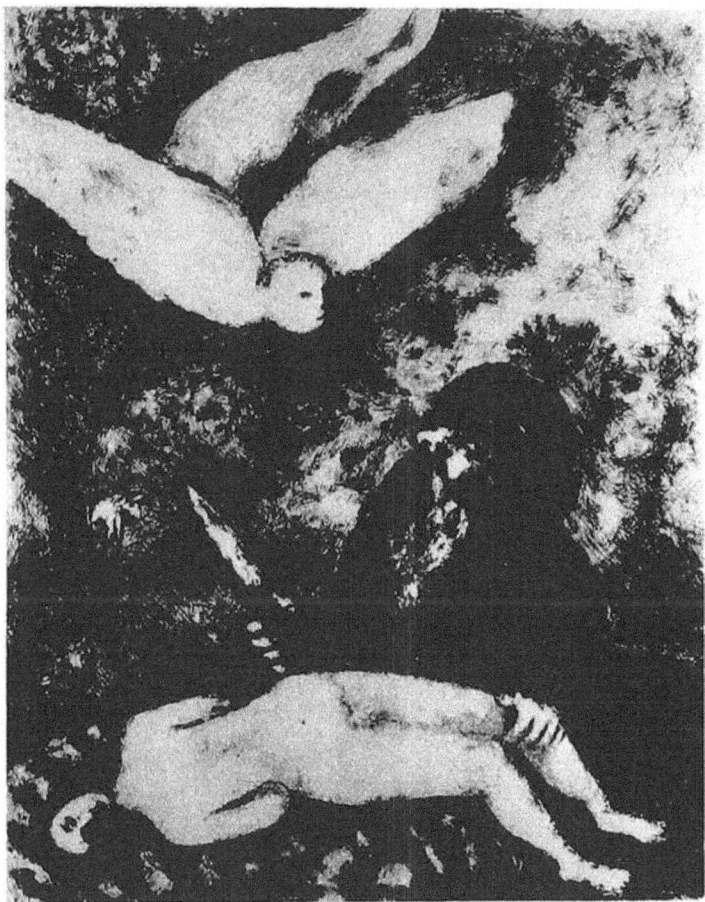

1. The Sacrifice of Isaac

2. Jacob's Return to Egypt

3. Moses' Investiture of Joshua

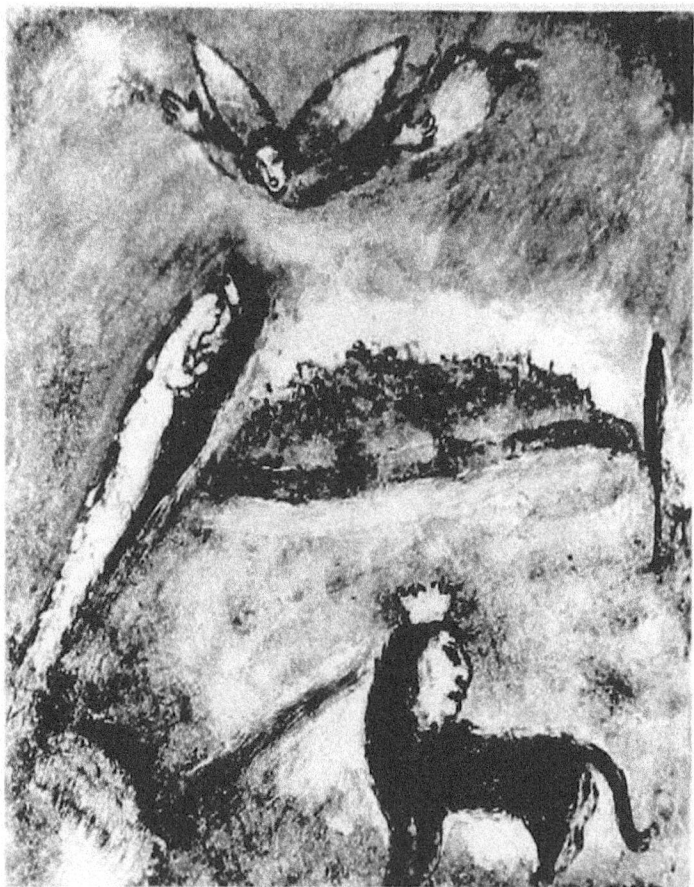

4. The Promise of Future Blessedness to Jerusalem

Chagall was certainly well aware—to Rembrandt's *The Return of the Prodigal Son*. In both cases, those who welcome and accept, i.e., the father and Joseph, do not look at the dear one who has been lost and is found. However, when in Rembrandt's picture the prodigal son hides his face on his father's breast, it is obvious that the old man's head, which is in the light and is slightly bowed, will look away over the head of his son. But when Benjamin in his jubilation darts towards his brother, he is not merely shown kneeling down before him, but his head, which is thrown upwards and turned towards his brother's face, and his arms, which are also reaching upwards, both clearly anticipate a meeting face to face. All the more surprising is it to find that although this Joseph embraces his brother tenderly, his eye does not see him, but—like the angels—sees only the unseen and the power that governs human destiny.

And just as the godhead in later times molds the destiny of the people through the operations of history, so from the beginning to the end of his career it guides the destiny of the Great Individual[3] through the double imperative of the Inner Voice and the demands of the world outside. This openness of the ego towards the call from without or from within leads to the fateful transformation in which the nature of man is realized. Man is required to fulfill the mission imposed upon him by the living power within himself, from which he is derived, into which he is flowing, and by which, too, his openness is continuously replenished.

3. [Cf. Neumann, *The Origins and History of Consciousness*, index, s.v.]

The purpose for which the individual is destined and the realization of that purpose can never in fact be separated from the mission in whose service he intervenes in the life of the collective, and it is actually bound up with the collective for good or ill. The individual always remains in this deeply rooted relationship with the collective, whether he leads it or misleads it, whether he appeals to it or exhorts it, or whether he simply expresses and shapes the dreams and myths of our common humanity. But the way in which this transpersonal power that encroaches upon the individual is at the same time his own innermost core and mover is given what is perhaps its most wonderful expression in Chagall's pictures of Moses.

The first of these (26), *The Discovery of the Infant Moses by the Princess*, is still entirely in the mythical realm, which, as so often with Chagall, merges into the atmosphere of fairy tale and the Jewish Haggada. The archetypal life of the "Divine Child" or the hero-child[4] begins, as so often in the life of mankind, with the miracle of his rescue from deadly peril and with the motif of the royal "adoptive mother." This first picture is followed immediately by the second (27), *The Call of Moses at the Burning Bush*. The scene of the Call is clearly portrayed here as a direct continuation of the mythical childhood; the second contains the purpose of the first—it was only because of the Call that this child was saved. Is it possible to represent the part played by

4. [Cf. in C. G. Jung and C. Kerényi, *Essays on a Science of Mythology*, tr. R.F.C. Hull (1949), the two essays on the Divine Child.]

destiny in the life of a man in a way which is less forced and more compelling than this direct sequence, in which the second scene follows on after the first? The Moses who is shown here at the Burning Bush is already an "old man." It is as if the long years that separate the infant in the little basket from the Moses kneeling before the bush which burns with the gloriole of the Divine Name were simply nonexistent. The young Moses, Moses the killer and refugee, and Moses the man are skipped as something purely provisional. It is only when we come to this scene in which he receives the divine call to his true self, to his quintessential being as an old man who is required to walk with God, that his real life, which is a continuation of his birth, begins.

But what a wonderful and at the same time simple Moses it is who is kneeling there before the gloriole and receiving his mission from God! No trace of the violence of his youth is to be found in him. It has been completely transformed into gentleness. He is as peaceful as the flocks that he tends as a shepherd, and the gentle dismay of this face reflects the narrative of the Bible, which tells us that Moses was "very meek, above all the men which were upon the face of the earth" (Num. 12:3). It is precisely the indescribable peacefulness of this face, the hand which Moses places in shocked surprise on his heart, and which so eloquently expresses to God his "I? Why I?!" —it is precisely this kneeling humility of an old man who has apparently already made his peace with God which now shines out in the light that is beginning to radiate from his head, and which is his real response to the threefold gloriole of the divine epiphany. And then there is the almost incredible change—the meeting between Moses and Aaron in the wilderness (28). This Moses, whom we see on the left, coming down from the mountain, walks like a man in a dream; he is in the trance brought on by his absorption in his mission and by the process of transformation in which his humble, anxious, skeptically denying ego has been melted away till nothing was left. His countenance is now exalted to the level of the daemonic; it is beyond all fear, yet the dark power which radiates from it inspires fear.

The figure of the priestly brother appears in the next two pictures (29 and 31) as a companion of Moses; then, however, it disappears, whereas the figure of Moses grows to monstrous size and his humanity recedes more and more behind the superhuman and inhuman attributes of his vocation. In the scene where he proclaims his mission before Pharaoh, the doll-like Pharaoh, he is a white adjuring flame; when the rod is changed into a serpent (30), he is a sorcerer with divine powers at whose command the serpent in a hissing arc towers gigantically beside the gigantic form of Moses himself, before a toy world which is beginning to reel and totter. But in the terrifying picture in which Moses is shown calling down darkness upon Egypt (31), he is no longer a human sorcerer but an incarnation of the godhead whose name hovers over him in the darkness. And just as, in the top corner of the plate, the hand of the angel who is portrayed gazing at the letters of the Divine Name blesses and evades Moses with a single gesture, so, in the bottom corner, a crouching priest-brother, at once reverent and afraid, looks up at the old man who dominates the picture and the darkness with the gigantic menace of his raised arm. This countenance of Moses, with its mingling of the divine and the numinously daemonic, evokes feelings of astonishment and dread. Nothing seems to be left of the deep humility of the face at the Burning Bush. All is dominated by the deadly power that governs the divine operations of destiny. However, the personality of the man who slew the Egyptian who had acted wrongfully is still very much alive, though radically transformed and exalted, in the suprapersonal gesture of the prophet dedicated to the mission of the godhead. Behind the paradoxical figure who slew in his passion for righteousness and the Moses who knelt in the gentleness of his peace, we glimpse the lightning of the godhead itself, which slays the first-born of the land of Egypt, but which reveals itself not in storm and tempest but in the gentlest murmurings of the wind.

And then there is the plate with the breaking of the Tables (39) after the reception of the Law on Mount Sinai and the return to the people, who, with the aid of Moses' priest-brother Aaron, had been unfaithful, and to the golden calf which they had set up. This picture of the accusation and the complaint against the people, against humanity and against man, is like the complaint and accusation of the godhead itself. The transformation of the peaceful and humble Moses of the Call into the superhuman figure of the Moses who accuses heaven and mankind in the picture of the Breaking of the Tables leads on finally to the picture of his death (41), which takes place entirely in the human realm. The immense effort that the prophet had made, involving the dissolution of his own ego in the process of transformation and the self-transcendence of his own temperament in the cause of the Divine Mission, which was also the deepest imperative of his own being, ultimately culminates in his death. Here the old man rests, stretched out on the mountain. He has laid aside the staff of the wanderer. Before him shines in glory the Promised Land, the land it was not granted to him to enter. Yet over his head there is a murmuring of the wind, and in the cloud above the dying man, for the only time in Chagall's illustrations of the Bible, the godhead, which is elsewhere invariably represented by its name, appears in its human form.

The death scene is actually followed by Moses' investiture of Joshua (42) [cf. fig. 3]; Moses had "laid his hands upon him" (Deut. 34:9). Moses gives the blessing, and at the same time "gives up"; he gives up his mission and he gives up his burden. His face is now sheer radiance, nothing more; it radiates kindness and liberation. He himself is "beyond" everything—but there is a power that emanates from him which will grip and transform the man who receives his blessing. For there is something more than the weak, tired, and dying man whose lackluster eye beholds the Promised Land from afar; there is the "Spirit of Moses," from which wisdom proceeds, but which is also the spirit that with stormy and belligerent energy carries through the mission of the godhead against all resistance, bursts the bonds of servitude, gives laws to Israel, guides the wandering people through the wilderness to their goal, and makes it possible for them to conquer the Promised Land.

The inexorability of the mission and of destiny and the inability of the human ego to escape from the suprapersonal power with which it is intimately connected and which encounters it in the form of the divine are two aspects of one and the same reality, both in the Bible itself and in Chagall's illustrations of it. The transpersonal turns out to be the innermost quintessence of the personal, even when it appears to the ego to be something "wholly other." The white light of the godhead is refracted in the prism of the human psyche and becomes visible as color in man's emotions and as compulsion in the power which he cannot avoid and which transforms him. It is this that constitutes the indescribable closeness between God and man, even when man is unaware of the fact and worships the godhead as a reality which is infinitely remote.

The difficulty which Chagall mentioned when he told us that in his work of illustrating the Bible he had to take care not to become involved in storytelling relates to this basic condition of human existence. The reality of human life invariably entails the inclusion of a suprahuman dimension. Thus, although the picture which is being created must always represent a living episode in the history of the individual and of his people, the artist must always simultaneously reveal the existence of an "eternal" dimension in which the godhead is a present and potent influence. This intimacy between the human and the divine, with its paradoxical remoteness and its unfathomable incomprehensibility, activates the tension from which all these Biblical personalities suffer, and which they experience as though it was something "outermost" which is entrusted to them as their innermost task.

It is precisely at this point that something of the old unliberated atmosphere of Jewish man during the Dark Ages still seems to have an effect, even on Chagall. That is why his portrayal of the spirit of the Old Testament does not always quite do justice to its subject. It is not often that the wide, unfettered airs of the country in which all these divine events took place blow through the pages of these illustrations. When this does happen, however, our hearts and the world expand together. The restriction of the divine dimension to the relationship between the divine and the human and the excessive strain that this imposes on man loses something of its monstrous character, and a new sense of freedom and relief becomes possible, even where, as in the unique plate depicting a false prophet who has been killed by a lion (82), nature herself has been enlisted entirely in the service of the godhead. In the middle of the picture, under a somber sky, a white-hot sun is blazing; the slain prophet lies stretched out, white-robed, upon the ground. The black silhouette of the lion, the bending palm tree, the gentle gaze of the donkey—in all these things, despite the cruelty and inexorability of the subject, a unity of the whole living realm becomes discernible, and although man exists as a responsible agent in the midst of this unity, it nevertheless does extend beyond him—and that in itself is a consolation. On the whole, the animals so beloved by Chagall do not seem to feel comfortable in the dark and hugely dynamic world of the events that take place between man and God. There is practically no landscape in this work of Chagall's—no mountains, no plains, no trees, no sea, and the magnificent black-and-white character of these illustrations is still somehow faintly reminiscent of the black-and-white ethos of later Judaism, which does not comprehend the colored opulence of the Bible. It is not often we find a genuine Palestinian landscape of such accomplished beauty as the one on the plate which illustrates the meeting between Elijah and the widow (83).

What is represented is invariably the psychic-spiritual world of man himself, within which the age-old and deeply rooted feeling of Jewish man for the closeness of God is very much alive; it is no longer the world of the Old Testament and not yet the newly discovered joy of the love of Jewish man for *this* world. So it is understandable that, apart from a few Bedouins, the people who bring life to these plates are the people of small-town Jewish life, the people who wear the caftan and the little Jewish skullcap. And in actual fact, what other apparel should these people wear? But the great men, the fathers, kings and prophets, are beyond the stage where they are bound up with something ancient or associated with something practically extinct. The scroll of the Law and the skullcap, the lion of the Ark of the Covenant and the Hasidic hat,[5] the Star of David and the shofar, are like details out of folklore; they are at the same time genuine and spurious, they are interpenetrated

5. [Hasidism (from Hebrew *hasid*, "pious") is a mystical movement founded in Poland in the eighteenth century by Israel Baal Shem Tov.—Tr. See also, for this and other Hebrew terms, Gershom Scholem, *Major Trends in Jewish Mysticism* (3rd ed., 1954), index.]

and assimilated by the real artistic treatment of the stories; yet the local color they provide is legitimate, insofar as it establishes the continuity of the Jewish people and of its essential nature. For the Ghetto Jews of these illustrations are a "folk," and this is the only way in which it is possible to represent Jewish people in the context of the Bible. Yet the spirit of this people is not intellectual and Talmudic but Hasidic. The numinously daemonic personalities of the Bible who are portrayed by Chagall and who "walk with God" have nothing in common with the rabbis and scholars of the Galluth or Exile, but a great deal in common with the mighty figures of the Hasidic zadikkim[6] and their dealings with God and with men. If we compare Chagall's figures with those of Rembrandt, it will become clear to us that the world of the cabala and of Hasidism, which was still strange to Rembrandt, was one of the deepest emotional and spiritual-psychic roots of Chagall's work. This world, from which Chagall himself sprang, provides the basis for his rendering of the greater and older reality of the Bible, which has never relinquished its hold on Jewish people and is in fact calling them back to itself today.

Just as in the Jewish faith *hesed* and *din*, mercy and judgment, are regarded as the basic attributes of the godhead, so too the real happening that unfolds before our eyes in these etchings is the confrontation between black and white within the world of mankind and of the relations between man and God.

Neither here nor in the Bible is the terribleness of God, the aspect of God revealed in his judgments, unduly pre-

6. ["Teachers"; from Hebrew *zadik*, "righteous."—Tr.]

dominant. It is true that the overwhelming power of
God does impose a single pattern on the whole picture,
and this overwhelming superiority of the divine force of
destiny, which is experienced as so fundamental by modern man, is not visibly relieved or disguised by any loving
I-Thou relationship between man and the godhead. Moreover, the divine attribute of mercy cannot be dissociated
from the divine superiority in power. Whether it is Jacob, Joseph, Moses, David, or the prophets, salvation—
even when it is a salvation overflowing with richness and
light—is always inseparably bound up with the darkness
of pain and ignorance and the tragic smallness of the
isolated ego, and also with what, as seen by that ego, is
the overwhelming power of evil. It is only after many
years have elapsed that the anxious eyes of the Joseph
who was sold naked into the darkness of an alien Egypt
dissolve into the wise and understanding eyes of the
Joseph who is portrayed at the recognition scene with
his brethren; and the unspeakable sorrow of his father
as he breaks down over Joseph's bloodstained coat only
brightens terribly late in the story into the smile of childlike happiness on the old man's face as he journeys into
Egypt on the dusky camel. Judgment is mercy, mercy is
judgment. One and the same happening may prove to be
unfathomable to man's present ego at any given moment,
and it may be only after a long process of change and
development in his destiny that what appears to be dark-
est and most judgmental can become transparent in its
nature as mercy and light. The bridge over this antithesis between light and darkness is simply faith in the indissoluble covenant between God and man. This cove-

nant is manifested not only outwardly in history and in the succession of the generations, but inwardly in the fateful involvement of each individual human being with the suprahuman power which lives within him and which is able to change, to shape, and to illumine his life. The remoteness and invisibility of the God who appears in Chagall's illustrations only in the gloriole of the Divine Name is more than compensated by the closeness and visibility of the happening that he precipitates in man himself. In man the preponderance of mercy over judgment is established not only by the sheer fact that he is able to exist, but also because this existence compels him to undergo a process of continual transformation, in which new forms of darkness are constantly revealing themselves to him as pregnant with light.

This involvement of the individual with the universal is given what is perhaps its most beautiful expression in the plate depicting the promise of future blessedness to Jerusalem, which has found favor with God once again (98) [cf. fig. 4]. Under a gray sky the holy city is shown in the background. Above her shines a radiance that is like a secret gloriole of the divine mercy. An angel with outstretched arms is flying down from the upper center of the picture towards a bridal couple, who are rising from the left. This image of the bridegroom and bride, which constantly recurs in Chagall's work, is the age-old symbol for the union of the soul with God, and of the people with the godhead. In it, the complete identity of the personal with the collective is realized. We see Zion, the City, the people, and mankind—but we also see the soul of the individual. Historically, mankind is like the eternal Jew—forever on its wanderings. Chagall's design for the symbol of the future messianic peace of mankind takes the form of a roundel (92), which, with its godhead soaring above and its animal-creatures scattered playfully around, is more like a picture of the Creation than of a realized final state of the world. But in the picture of the Promise to Jerusalem, with its ascending pair of bridegroom and bride, this final goal, this end of time, is actually realized. Here there is no more wandering and no more history. Here everything has come to its appointed end, future is present, present future, and the collective is identical with the individual soul, which, as it ascends in its *hieros gamos* with the godhead, is redeemed. The crowned lion standing in the foreground of this picture of faith, the Lion of Judah, is represented with the face of Marc Chagall.

III

GEORG TRAKL:
THE PERSON AND THE MYTH

I

This study of Trakl does not attempt to interpret his poetry as a whole; instead, it concentrates on a single problem, the central problem of his life and poetry—the figure of the sister.

The sister and the sisterly quality in connection with the figure of the mother form the archetypal background of Trakl's existence—but not of his existence only: it is also to be found at the center of the creative existence and work of a whole group of creative artists. The Great Goddesses, uniting as they do the mother and daughter, the old and the young feminine principle, are the clearest expression we possess of the archetypes of the Great Feminine;[1] the need to remain in relationship with these archetypes for better or for worse is one of the central problems of the creative artist.

We have referred in another connection[2] to the close

"Georg Trakl: Person und Mythos," *Der schöpferische Mensch* (Zurich, 1959).

   1. See my *The Great Mother*, passim.
   2. See my *The Origins and History of Consciousness*, pp. 201-2.

GEORG TRAKL

connection between the "anima" figure and the sister. The release of the anima from the power of the mother, the liberation of the "young feminine" whom the man can marry from the domination of the "Great Mother" or "old feminine" principle, is one of the most crucial tasks of the "hero," whose deeds represent all masculine development. Even in a normal masculine development the power of the "Great Mother" archetype is by no means negligible and its conquest is rich in crisis. It is only by living through a slow process of personality transformation that a man can replace his mother-fixation by an attachment to his sister, who belongs to his own generation; and it is only after this connection in its turn has been conquered that he can achieve a real relationship with a sexual partner. Yet the old attachments are never simply "extinguished"; they are transformed and then their life continues. The decisive point in this context is that in a normal development the incest taboo is not violated. A fixation to the personal mother and sister is no longer the determining factor, but the maternal and sisterly qualities are preserved in an archetypal form as a universal human constituent in the man's relationship to a living woman.

This means that the prepersonal archetypal dependence of the infant, which owing to its undeveloped ego is not yet able to relate to persons, is relieved by the personalization of the attachment to the mother, which is the prototype of all personal attachments. After the personal attachment to the sister has been formed, both of these ties, and especially their sexual components, are to a great extent repressed. It is only after this repression has taken place that a man can achieve a personal attachment to a partner, which may then contain more or less powerful elements of the archetypal figures of the mother and sister.

In the case of the creative artist, however, the prepersonal archetypal attachment remains largely intact and frequently reinforces the personal attachment to the mother and sister. The double figure of the "Goddesses," which represents the transpersonal unity of the "Great Feminine" archetype of mother and daughter, is alive and active in his psyche. It is for this reason that the "personal" attachments of the normal development retain an archetypal resonance in the creative artist, so that the personal element in the encounter recedes in favor of the archetypal. The result is that the "inner" feminine and the "image" which represents it are often more vital to him than the personal feminine itself. Even so, the incest taboo is still obeyed, to the extent that the overwhelming power of the archetypal as a transpersonal force excludes a sexual relationship with the personal figures of the mother and sister, however formative the influence of these figures may be.

Trakl's divergent development is something more than a special case in which the unity of personal and transpersonal archetypal relationships is demonstrated with unusual clarity in all its fate-determining power. It also, in our view, opens up a deep insight into the nature of "incest" and the significance of the incest taboo.

When the mother-anima archetype is constellated in a creative way, and especially when this constellation is overstressed, the totality of the psyche and the multiplicity of the archetypal world are set in motion. It is for this reason that an abundance of archetypal material is demonstrated in Trakl's poetry. The really decisive point, however, is the way in which this material is constellated and the relationship of coordination in which it stands to the poet's own fateful development. We must adopt a genetic approach if we are to realize how parts of the archetypal world appear in a temporal sequence whose order is determined by the nature of the material concerned; in other words, it is the coordination of archetypally conditioned phases of development[3] which enables us to distinguish what is "progressive" and what "regressive," what is to be regarded as healthy and what as sick in the context of normal human development. This genetic approach makes it possible for us to realize how the unity of the transpersonal and the personal dimensions produces the unique fate of a human individual. Only when we grasp how the universal human archetype coalesces with the uniqueness of the individual and of the personal environment that belongs uniquely to him does it become clear whether and in what way the mythic realm of the powers of the unconscious background appears in the unique figures of mother and sister, father and brother, whether it is dominant or recessive in them, or becomes repressed, or invades the personal world of the individual. Our real task in this paper is to demonstrate the relationship between person and myth through the unity of fate and poetry in Georg Trakl.[4]

3. Ibid., passim.
4. It was not until after I had completed this essay that I first saw Heinrich Goldmann's book *Katabasis: Eine tiefenpsychologische Studie zur Symbolik der Dichtungen Georg Trakls* (Trakl-Studien, IV; Salzburg, 1957). In this valuable study Goldmann

In view of the fact that this essay relates specifically to the relationship between personal and transpersonal factors in Trakl's poetry, a brief biographical note on Trakl is required at this stage.[5] In its major task of elucidating Trakl's personality, and also in its discussion of his illness and its relationship to his work as a poet, Spoerri's study seems to me to have been largely successful. However, there are a number of points in which I differ from his interpretation, and as these are essential to my argument, it will be necessary to mention them in this context.

Spoerri takes the view that Trakl's childhood had been

---

examines Trakl's symbolism by applying the method of amplification as practiced in analytical psychology; naturally, in this way he frequently arrives at analogous interpretations, while at the same time, by examining the symbolism in detail in accordance with the scope and intention of his inquiry, he reaches some illuminating conclusions. However, since he only amplifies and does not take into consideration the genetic approach to the problem, his treatment falls short at the very point that is the focus of interest in my essay—namely, the demonstration of the fateful unity of person and myth in the life and poetry of Georg Trakl. This unity, and with it, too, the unity of Trakl's poetry in itself, becomes transparent when we grasp the central significance of the mother-sister relationship for Trakl's life and work and realize that this relationship forms the axis around which—for better or for worse—the world revealed by Trakl's poems is in fact organized.

5. These remarks are based largely on Theodor Spoerri's excellent study, *Georg Trakl, Strukturen in Persönlichkeit und Werk* (Bern, 1954), and on vol. iii of the Gesammelte Werke, *Nachlass und Biographie*, edited by W. Schneditz (Salzburg, 1949).

"normal," and that it was not until the onset of puberty that a "kink" developed in his lifeline. Yet apart from the fact that we know that distorted development and psychic deviation of the kind from which Trakl suffered derive generally, to a large extent, from developmental disturbances at a very early age, there are two stories from Trakl's own childhood whose meaning is quite unmistakable.

It is said that as a boy Trakl was easily excitable, even to the point of fury. In itself, this might still be within the bounds of a normal reaction of defiance; however, the same cannot be said of another story, according to which, ostensibly from "hatred of any unduly rapid movement," he once as a child "threw himself in front of a black horse that was shying, and tried to do the same on the railway, to stop the movement of a train."[6] Still more horrible is the story that as a child of approximately eight years of age he "walked into a pond, and only his big hat, which was floating on the water, revealed the spot where he had disappeared and from which he had to be rescued."[7] Spoerri's comment on this incident, that it proved "how early in his life he showed a tendency to dreaminess and absentmindedness," is completely beside the point. Behavior such as this is entirely beyond the limits of normality, whether we interpret it as unconscious suicide or as a tendency observable in earliest youth to return to the maternal element or to extinction. This well-attested incident is clear evidence of an underlying psychotic situation, all the more so since we know how difficult a suicide of this

6. Spoerri, p. 23.   7. Ibid.

kind actually is, or in other words how strong the power of the inner yearning "to get into the water" must have been in Trakl, even as a child. A remark made by Trakl late in his life, to the effect that "up to his twentieth year he had noticed nothing except water in the outside world"[8] and his saying "I am only half-born, after all"[9] point in the same direction. Trakl wishes to return totally to the water, that maternal abode of the unconscious from which he has only been half delivered: in this way the central motif of Trakl's life, which is in fact his craving for death, has already been sounded, loud and clear.

In Trakl's case, it is really out of the question to talk about a "normal" childhood, though it was only later, with the onset of puberty, that the profound disorder of the personality from which he suffered became apparent to those around him. How little they were aware of this childhood of his, overshadowed as it was by his feeling that he had been rejected by his mother, comes out clearly in an account of him given by a relative and reported by Spoerri: "We are told that as a boy he was high-spirited, unruly, and healthy, like his brothers and sisters."[10] Yet the eleven-year-old who is described by Spoerri as "a sunny youngster, pleasant and game for all kinds of tricks" was a failure at school, and later on, at puberty, his disturbed condition was obvious even to the unaware people around him.

The fact that Trakl, together with five of his friends, played a leading part in a so-called "society of poets" may look at first like a piece of normal development;

8. Ibid., p. 31.   9. Ibid.   10. Ibid., p. 23.

however, even this becomes problematical when we are told that "a young man who belonged to this association castrated himself for religious reasons."[11] How it came about that Trakl's "habits" at this period, and the incidents to which these habits gave rise, never caused his parents sufficient disquiet to induce them even to consult a doctor completely baffles understanding.

At the age of fifteen Trakl was already smoking to excess cigarettes that had been steeped in opium; he was also drugging himself with chloroform. "It was not simply that he was taking chloroform at home; he used to carry a little flask of this narcotic around with him, and it was a frequent occurrence for his friends to find him, in winter, half-stupefied and frozen on the Kapuzinerweg."[12] The picture is completed by the information that he followed this up by "drinking wine copiously and with relish" and that even his peculiar poetic colleagues were alarmed by his repeated threats to commit suicide. He had already once missed his promotion from the seventh class at school, which implies a serious difficulty in learning, and when this happened for the second time he left school and became—an apprentice pharmacist. In his biography, Schneditz tells us, "There was a special reason why his parents were not particularly pleased by this choice and in fact actually opposed it."[13] We can only express our astonishment at this cool observation by Trakl's biographer, which reflects the attitude of his parents. It was a known fact that Trakl had

11. Ibid., p. 24.
12. Ibid. [The Kapuzinerweg is a street in Salzburg.]
13. Schneditz, vol. III, p. 74.

become addicted to chloroform through his "friendship" with a pharmacist, and he naturally chose the same profession for himself, since this was the easiest way in which he could obtain access to narcotics. Abuse of alcohol and cigarettes and addiction to opium, chloroform, and barbituric acid were the results. Addiction to cocaine also seems well-established; abuse of mescaline is improbable.

Trakl's family background, which is described by his biographers as pleasant and middle-class, was actually catastrophic and exposed Trakl to mortal danger. Even Spoerri, who produces all the evidence, fails to evaluate it correctly. Trakl's mother and three of his siblings were subject to addictions. His father is described by his biographer as "benevolent"; there is a reference to his fleshy nose, and we are told that "on a picture of his father as an old man his face, with its slit eyes and its long, straight beard, is almost reminiscent of a Chinese sage."[14] We hear, too, of the affluence of the family and of the "art treasures" in their flat—in fact the whole picture is clearly intended to depict a heroic background—yet strangely enough there is no mention of any initiative undertaken by his father or indeed of any attempt on his part to give his son the slightest assistance in the desperate situation in which he found himself. Characteristically, in Trakl's work the figure of the father remains almost completely in the background. The fact that Trakl reacted depressively to his father's death is entirely understandable: it is by no means necessarily an expression of "love," as his biographer prefers to call it. We

14. Ibid., p. 68.

know how frequently depression can be a symptom of repressed aggression, and who can dispute that this unhappy and suffering son had every reason to hate the father who had done nothing to counteract his son's terrible self-destruction, either by representing for him a world of collective values or by a personal relationship of any kind, and had actually deserted him just as much as his mother had?

Evidence for the rose-colored optimism that is typical of this biography is to be found in the remark, "He was inconsolable when his father died in 1910,"[15] and still more in the continuation of the same sentence: "And although, as he himself admitted on more than one occasion, he had been a source of grave anxiety to his mother, he remained linked to her by a bond of reverent and grateful love till the day of his death. An army postcard, written to her only a few weeks before he died, still survives to bear witness to this relationship." We can just picture this Austrian family romance. Trakl's own statement that "there were times when he had hated his mother so much that he could have murdered her with his own hands"[16] and the terrible figure of the mother in his poems tell a very different story.

Trakl's incest with his beloved sister, "the most beautiful girl, the greatest artist, and the strangest woman he had ever known,"[17] took place during the dangerous period of puberty. His relationship with her was and remained the central relationship of his life, and the severe crisis that Trakl underwent after his sister's marriage is not an "enigma," as Spoerri calls it. Apart from

15. Ibid., p. 69.   16. Spoerri, p. 42.   17. Ibid., p. 39.

trifling experiences with prostitutes and a strange, half-perverse, half-platonic relationship with one old prostitute,[18] there was no woman in Trakl's life besides his sister.

Trakl's cult of Nietzsche, his youthful veneration for Wagner, and his approval of the glorification of incest in Wagner's *Die Walküre* are no more than rationalizations for the fateful and fatal attachment between this brother and sister. This found expression not only in Trakl's plan for a suicide pact with his sister[19] but also in the close bond that actually led her, after her brother's death, to share his fate. Obviously owing to Trakl's influence, she too became subject to addictions, and in spite of her talent, her career as a pianist was a failure, as was her marriage. Characteristically, after her brother's death she spent the money she had inherited from him on narcotics, and after two unsuccessful abstinence cures she committed suicide. She too seems to have been the victim of a disintegration of the personality, though in her case the symptoms were of a different type. Hysterical states, drunkenness, sexual instability, and a general eccentricity without real creative content complete the picture of this pathological person, who meant "everything" to Trakl.

While his relationship with his sister remained dominant throughout his life and she was obviously always the person closest to him, his relationship with his mother, which was so vital to his poetry, played no part at all in his outer life. She is said to have been impulsive and unpredictable, obstinate and impossible to fathom,

18. Ibid., p. 41.   19. Ibid.

deficient in maternal warmth towards the children and more concerned about her collection of antique glass than about anything else. "She felt that she was not understood by her husband, her children, and in fact the whole world,"[20] and she was herself a drug addict. Apart from his sister, Trakl had no more real relationship with any other person than he had with his own mother.

Trakl's narcissism, which was so extreme that it amounted to "a feeling that his body was untouchable,"[21] his aggressiveness, which went so far that an infuriated friend is said to have fired a shot at him, his sadomasochism, his anxieties, his guilt feelings, and the whole pathological structure of his personality and his reactions do not concern us here. Spoerri has described these characteristics exhaustively in the context of their relationship to the personality and work of Trakl. It will be sufficient for our purpose to quote his summary: "The presence of a crowd was so disturbing to Trakl that he only frequented empty inns, among which he was especially fond of the cheap, rural variety, where he would lean both elbows on a broad table. If at all, it was only at night, when wine had given him confidence, that he ventured into the livelier parts of the city where, as Buschbeck tells us,[22] he used to stare with malevolent eyes into a large coffeehouse. When his work as a pharmacist involved serving customers, this made him so acutely anxious that in a single morning he saturated six shirts with perspiration; similarly, when in the sum-

20. Ibid.   21. Ibid., p. 31.
22. [Erhard Buschbeck, *Georg Trakl* (Berlin, 1917).]

mer of 1914 he wished to withdraw from the bank a sum of money that had been made payable to him,[23] he was suddenly overwhelmed by panic. As Buschbeck says, "Loathing and fear are two emotions which he cannot overcome." He gave up traveling by public transport because he felt so constricted by the presence of the other passengers; he thought a fire wall was a grinning void, often stayed away from a restaurant because he was terrified of the waiter, and even the harmless smile of a bureaucrat might suddenly turn, as he looked at it, into the coarse grimace of the doorkeeper of a brothel. One incident that struck bystanders as particularly grotesque took place at a fair, when, in the midst of all the music and dancing, he suddenly gazed with horror at a calf's head which had been offered as a prize and, trembling all over, exclaimed, "That is our Lord Jesus!"[24]

Yet it was not until he was exposed to the hellish environment of the war that Trakl's personality, with its strange combination of hypersensitivity and crude strength, finally broke down under the strain. After the battle of Grodek—though he was not a doctor and was in fact entirely unaided—he was required to look after ninety severely wounded men who were quartered in a barn. One of these men committed suicide in Trakl's presence. Others died screaming, and we are told that in front of the barn "deserters who had been hanged were dangling from the trees."[25]

23. [This was the 20,000 crowns made over to Trakl in July 1914 by Ludwig Wittgenstein, who admired his poems. See *Selected Poems*, Editor's Note, p. 7 (cited in n. 36 below).]

24. Spoerri, p. 32. 25. Ibid.

Under the pressure of this terrible burden the unity of Trakl's personality, which was held together with such pain and difficulty, came very near to the point of collapse. He leaped to his feet before the eyes of his comrades and tried to shoot himself with his revolver. His weapon was taken away from him and he calmed down. This suicidal episode may not at first sight appear to have been such an unmitigated disaster; initially, Trakl seems to have recovered from it. But the event proves that it would be a mistake to interpret this attempt as "not serious" simply because he made it in the presence of his comrades. The truth is that this was the first sign of the onset of his final alienation from reality. Trakl was recalled to the base hospital for an examination of his mental condition. The result was that he was seized by a phobia that he might be court-martialed and shot as a deserter—a phobia which never left him for the rest of his life.[26] He was actually diagnosed as a schizophrenic, but as he was suffering from an angina at the time he was detained in a cell which was also occupied by an officer in a state of alcoholic delirium. A friend who visited him and wished to remove him for private treatment was refused permission to do so. When he died, on 3 November 1914, the cause of death was given as "cardiac paralysis." In fact, however, as was admitted later, he died of an overdose of cocaine. It was not possible to establish whether this was a case of suicide or of an accidental overdose.

The final disintegration of Trakl's personality was

26. The deep symbolic meaning of this fear will become apparent only at the end of this essay.

precipitated by the shock of his war experience; there can be no doubt, however, that long before this period and quite apart from his various addictions Trakl was a mentally sick person. The heroic achievement of Trakl's life was his success in wringing from his severely disturbed and increasingly threatened personality an output of poetic work which, for all its uniqueness and strangeness, still remained so far grounded in our common humanity that its creation opened up a new world to our experience.

3

It is not often that the personal tragedy of an artist is so clearly exposed as it is in the case of Trakl; it is not often, either, that his personal complexes and his pathological disposition—whether the latter is aggravated by fate or conditioned by his constitution—are so conspicuous, as it were, to the naked eye. Yet what makes Trakl's work and personality so illuminating is precisely the fact that this work and the whole world of his poetry, in all its unique strangeness and despite its connection with the poet's personal life and fate, assumed a form which is transpersonal and possesses universal validity. As the poet's life approached its end—when he was twenty-seven years old—his poetry and the world that it portrayed changed from a "real" dimension experienced in poetical terms to the shaping of a mythic reality which becomes more and more transparent. As this transformation is carried through, the world and everything within it that has life becomes pregnant with symbolic meaning;

it transcends the narrowly "real" dimension of everything concrete and personal and passes beyond it into a
genuine reality of its own, which is in fact the unitary
reality that underlies all things.[27]
Even if Trakl's early poetry is already overshadowed
by horror, we nevertheless find in him the "beautiful
world" seen in terms of the simple, concrete world. Even
where the poetry is full of melancholy, it is still contained within the boundaries of the real and its tone and
coloring never completely lose their objective, represen-
tational character.

Rondel[28]

Melted and gone is the gold of the days
The evening's brown and blue shades:
The soft flute-notes of the shepherd died.
The evening's blue and brown shades;
Melted and gone is the gold of the days.

This tone of reality remains, it does not disappear later
on, but the color of the melancholy changes with the
color of the world. Let us now contrast this poem with
another:

Song of a Captive Blackbird[29]

Dark breath in the green branches
Little blue flowers sway around the face

27. See my "Die Erfahrung der Einheitswirklichkeit" ("The
Experience of the Unitary Reality"), Eranos-Jahrbuch, XXIV
(1955).
28. G. Trakl, Die Dichtungen (Salzburg, 1938). [Where this is
given as the source of a poetic quotation, the translation is by
Eugene Rolfe.]
29. "Gesang einer gefangenen Amsel," Dichtungen, p. 171.

Of the Lonely One and his golden step
Dying away beneath the olive tree.
Up flutters Night on a drunken wing.
So gently bleeds humility,
Dew that drops slowly from blossoming thorn.
Compassion with her radiant arms
Cradles a breaking heart.

We are tempted to conclude that what is portrayed
here is no longer the "world" in the normal sense of the
term, but a "psychic reality." Yet an interpretation along
these lines would miss an essential element in the picture, that is to say, the firm attachment to this world
which survives in every detail, the concreteness of all this
actual reality which is visible and tangible, here and now.
The "dew that drops slowly from blossoming thorn" is
visible reality; yet this dimension of the real on a concrete level is totally transformed, since it becomes at the
same time a symbol and a parable for something quite
different—for a "gently bleeding humility." Here one
thing does not stand side by side with another, nor does
one thing stand for another thing, but, in a magically
dreamlike way, both things are one. Humility *bleeds*;
here humility is not expressed in terms of concepts but
concretely—it is a humility which has a heart and which
can suffer from a wound. At the same time, however,
the world of the visible merges into the world of sound
and music, since in the verse "So gently bleeds humility"
a genuine fusion has been achieved between the realms
of sensation, feeling and ideas. This then dies away in
the second, closely related verse, "Dew that drops slowly
from blossoming thorn," so that both have found their

place at the same time in the dimension of the real, outside world. In spite of the dreamlike effect produced by the juxtaposition of these two verses, the concreteness of the details and of the associations which float around them remains intact. The thorn is certainly blossoming, yet at the same time it is a thorn with which both bleeding and dropping remain vitally connected. But in "gently" and even more in "so gently," the essential nature of humility is revealed to us, in its uncomplaining quietness and quiet endurance.

The introductory verse, "Dark breath in the green branches," still seems to denote a simple piece of external reality. Yet the greenness of the branches is rendered nocturnal by the darkness of the breath and in this way an element of fateful estrangement enters the verse; at the same time the phrase "dark breath," in which "breath" in the original is expressed by the unusual word "Odem," achieves an almost mythical resonance. The music of the vowels in the five words "Dunkler Odem in grünen Gezweig,"[30] in conjunction with the abrupt breaking off of the sentence at the end of the verse, evokes a landscape that is as magnificent as it is transcendental—a landscape worthy of El Greco. It is only in the luminous glow of this landscape that the strange "little blue flowers" come to have a meaning. They "sway around the face of the Lonely One" and around his "golden step dying away beneath the olive tree." Yet this Grecoesque scene from Gethsemane is overshadowed by something even more uncanny, something alien and daemonic which, as though triumphing and at the same time

30. ["Dark breath in the green branches," ibid.]

poisoning the air, darkens the light power of the golden step and of the face around which the little blue flowers sway: "Up flutters Night on a drunken wing." In this brief verse which is, as it were, immediately dropped, "Night" appears in the mythical form of a gigantic bird whose black wings darken the world. Side by side with this mighty mythical element, something daemonically evil, expressed in the fluttering motion and in the strange "drunken" quality of this abrupt transition, whirs up at the same time. But beyond this daemonic darkness that reels over the world there is a living realm which is completely untouched by it: "So gently bleeds humility, / Dew that drops slowly from blossoming thorn." In this verse, which is—we take it—essentially a paraphrase of Jesus on the Mount of Olives accepting his fate, the suffering of the man who accepts his fate merges with the transfiguration of the man who dies. However, not a word of this is expressed explicitly or in any way pinned down; everything is left suspended, as it were, in a stream of sound, color, and meaning. Humanity suffers under the dark drunkenness of the power that overshadows the world, but the thorn of its suffering does blossom, and in the breakthrough of the final verses— "compassion with her radiant arms / Cradles a breaking heart"—suffering and death are overcome in a transfiguration that is unique in Trakl's work.

How is it possible to understand this poem in terms of Trakl's closeness to the figure of Jesus, who for him is the only man that possesses the "face of man," if at the same time the poem appears under the strange title of "Song of a Captive Blackbird"? Is this the complaint of the

bird, of the human soul, or of the world soul? In the
unity of everything that ultimately belongs together,
which we have described as the "unitary reality,"[31] there
is no contradiction between these different interpretations. The blackbird is a blackbird in the reality of a
world of which Trakl speaks in another poem:[32]

> . . . On the hill the evening wind drops gently,
> The blackbird's lament grows dumb,
> And the soft flutes of autumn
> Are silent in the reeds.

But the blackbird is also the soul-bird of myth, dream,
and fairy tale, and because it is a blackbird in the world
of the evening wind and at the same time a blackbird in
the world of the soul, it sings its lament as the soul of
the world.

The unity of outer and inner, of the lament of the
blackbird and the lament of the soul, which is realized
in this poem, is seen with unusual clarity when in all its
sadness it stands in relief against the very different world
of the day, in which the light of the sun forces everything that is real into the inordinate brightness of an
existence that is unbearable because it is divided and no
longer unitary. So the soul laments in the "Dark calls
of the blackbird" and in the "Seven Song of Death":[33]

> Bluish wanes the spring, under sucking trees
> A dark thing wanders into evening and decline,

31. [See Neumann, "Man and Transformation," in *Art and the
Creative Unconscious*, p. 175.]
32. "Geistliche Dämmerung" ("Holy Dusk"), *Dichtungen*, p.
135.
33. Ibid., pp. 146, 138.

Listening to the blackbird's soft lament,
Silent the Night appears, a bleeding deer,
Which sinks down slowly on the hill.

The psychic is always something that laments and is melancholy, something soft, humble, suffering and declining, something that is strange and alien in the world of the day, since "The soul is a stranger upon earth."[34] At the same time, declining (as of the sun) is not identical with death but with evening and with a transition into the blueness of the nocturnal, in which another and deeper reality is alive.

Wherever existence is unable to live in this unity of the real and is separated from it, melancholy, lament for what has been lost, and unquenchable yearning appear on the scene. This yearning of Trakl's, which—not only in him—is the deepest source of the passion that drives him to "addiction," belongs with an existence in the world that is experienced essentially as an existence in a strange land. That is why he tells us that "the soul is a stranger upon earth" and it is for this reason, too, that the "stranger," whether male or female, is such a basic figure in Trakl's poetry. This element of alienation becomes more and more pronounced in Trakl's poetry. His youthful poems are still full of the experience of this world, however gloomy and uncanny that experience may be. Images of reality and of a world-ego that experiences them occupy the foreground, even if the music of these poems is filled to the brim with melancholy and lament. It is true that poems relating to the world in this extraverted way occur in Trakl's later work and poems of

34. Ibid., p. 147.

"estrangement" are to be found in his early period, but
the main emphasis in Trakl's life and work shifts ap-
preciably, as time goes on, in the direction of the world
of mythical alienation.

When Trakl is aware of the possibility of fulfillment
on earth, this takes the form of a life lived in communion with the countryside. Such closeness to nature is
contrasted with the crowded congestion of life in the
cities, to which the following verses pointedly apply:

A thorny wilderness entwines the city[35]

and

Oh, the great city's madness when at nightfall
The crippled trees gape by the blackened wall,
The spirit of evil peers from a silver mask;
Lights with magnetic scourge drive off the stony night.
Oh, the sunken pealing of evening bells.[36]

On the other hand, the poem entitled "The Beautiful
City,"[37] which begins with the verse "Ancient squares
sunnily silent," paints a contrary picture of the medieval
city, in which the unity of everything that is living almost seems to have been preserved intact.

The symbol for this unspoiled beautiful and holy
reality, which is being, or has already been, lost in the

35. Ibid., p. 195.
36. *Selected Poems G. Trakl*, ed. Christopher Middleton, tr.
Robert Grenier, Michael Hamburger, David Luke, and Christopher Middleton (London, 1968), p. 81, "To the Silenced" (M.H.).
[With quotations from this source, the translator's initials are
given.]
37. "Die Schöne Stadt," *Dichtungen*, p. 16.

process of the evolution of modern man, is the united duality of "bread and wine." Contemporary man, who has fallen under the curse of evil, and who, both wittingly and unwittingly, is living in the empty and loud despair of the godless, has lost this holy reality:

Despair, sad night of thought, despair high-arching;
Eve's shadow falls, halloo of hunt, red coin consigned.
Cloud, broken by light, the Supper's end;
This bread, this wine, have silence in their keeping.[38]

The symbol of bread and wine, which occurs repeatedly in Trakl, contains a conscious echo of Hölderlin's great poem, in the first part of which the basic motifs of Trakl's own poetry and life—night, madness, and drunkenness—are sounded. The West, Trakl's own civilization, is losing this world, which is falling into a state of decay and disintegration owing to the onesided "rationalization" of the conscious mind. In Trakl himself, however, it is for a different reason that bread and wine, as a symbol of lived reality, recedes more and more into the background. It is because he is dominated by the completely different and alien dimension of a mythical existence. When we hear the notes of the "Spiritual Song":[39]

In the village life is kind,
Gardener mows by ancient walls,
Hark! The organ softly calls,
Mingling sound and golden shine,

38. "Mankind," *Selected Poems*, p. 13 (C.M.).
39. "Geistliches Lied," *Dichtungen*, p. 20.

Sound and shine,
Love here hallows bread and wine.

when we are told:

And bread and wine are sweet from hard toil's pains.[40]

or when we read the final stanza of the wonderful poem
entitled: "Soul of Autumn":[41]

God, to thy gentle hands commending
Bread and wine, our true life's gain
Man submits his own dark ending,
All his guilt and crimson pain.

—in all these cases the poet's concern is with a genuine
world conceived in terms of existence in a fulfilled and
therefore consecrated reality of which Trakl himself
never lost sight, although he was less and less able to
realize it in his own life. But this loss in his own personal
life is bound up with the fact that his world-ego, that
part of his ego which was related to an external and
human reality, is progressively replaced by a mythical
ego. The anonymity of this other ego diminishes the
boundaries of Trakl's world-ego and of his personality
as a whole and in so doing prepares the way for the
emergence of a changed, alienated, immensely powerful,
and in every way overwhelming reality. The anonymity
of the power that expresses itself in this form is more and
more estranged and remote from what initially appears
as Trakl's own poetic ego. From this distance, the poetry
now no longer speaks of an ego that belongs to the poet
but only of "that man," the stranger, the Lonely One.

40. Ibid., p. 28.   41. Ibid., p. 122.

The loss of this ego is identical with the extinction of his face. So we read, for example:

> But as I descended the rocky path, madness seized hold of me and I cried out aloud in the night; and as with silvery fingers I leaned over the silent waters, I saw that my countenance had forsaken me.[42]

At the same time, however, and as a direct result of this change, Trakl becomes a poet in the archaic sense of the term—that is to say, a man in whom and through whom the song of the world itself is sung:

> Dark mouth, you are mighty
> Within, figure formed
> Out of autumn clouds,
> Golden evening stillness.[43]

This dark mouth at the heart of the golden evening stillness, which is actually the mouth of the blue world itself, becomes a song in the poet, even when, as an ego, he is increasingly silenced and declining, and is losing himself more and more in the world of a derangement or mental darkness that perhaps reveals its true and secret meaning in Trakl more than in any other poet.

From the very beginning traces can be detected in Trakl's poetry of this change, which finally fulfills itself in the later poems. It runs parallel with a development in his personality, which had been disturbed from the days of his earliest childhood, and had then, at puberty, culminated in a break in the maturation of his ego, as a

42. Ibid., p. 192.
43. Ibid., "Die Schwermut" ("Melancholy"), p. 181.

result of which the normal and necessary transformation of the ego at puberty was experienced only as a loss of the childish ego and a birth into the world as a place of guilt.

The onset of this personal crisis at puberty is intimately connected with the catastrophe of Trakl's incest with his sister. What this catastrophe meant for Trakl far transcended anything we could categorize as a personal feeling of guilt. It is only when the meaning of the sister in the context of Trakl's poetry and Trakl's world as a whole has become approximately clear in our minds that we can attempt anything like an adequate appraisal of what actually took place in this crucial collision between Trakl and the world.

Traces of the occurrence of this incest can be detected in many passages in Trakl's poetry. But because this was not a case of an unconscious wish but of an actual happening and because in spite of it the relationship between the brother and sister remained exceedingly close, its meaning is crucial and provides us with a key to the understanding of Trakl's world. The way in which in this context the personal realm always turns out to be inseparably bound up with a transpersonal dimension is one of the mysteries of Trakl's poetry, and even if we cannot hope to solve the enigma, we can still try to enter into it sympathetically with our feelings and in this way to bring it nearer to our understanding.

For Trakl, the loss of childhood was more than the loss of a world; it was the final loss of any possibility of living at all, since for him life meant the possibility of living in innocence. The perfect expression of this "living

in innocence" and of the loss of his childlike piety from
which Trakl never recovered is to be found in the "Caspar Hauser Song":[44]

> He truly adored the sun, as, crimson, it sank from
>   the hill-top,
> The paths of the forest, the blackbird singing
> And the joy of green.
>
> Serious was his habitation in the tree-shade
> And pure his face.
> God spoke a gentle flame into his heart:
> O man!
>
> His silent footstep found the city at evening;
> The dark lament of his mouth:
> I want to be a horseman.
>
> But bush and beast pursued him,
> House and twilight garden of pallid men
> And his murderer sought him.
>
> Beautiful the spring and summer and the autumn
> Of the righteous man, his soft footfall
> Beside the dark rooms of dreamers.
> By night he stayed alone with his star;
>
> Saw snow falling through bare branches
> And in the dusking hall his murderer's shadow.
>
> Silver it fell, the head of the not-yet-born.

In this poem the wholeness of a life considered as the
unity of day and night and also as the complete life of
the year assumes visible form before our eyes. The sun

44. *Selected Poems*, p. 59 (D.L.).

and the forest, the joy of green and the city at evening, and at the same time the course of life from spring to winter are here revealed as fulfilled reality and wholeness. But an essential part of the picture is a man whose autumn is called "the autumn of the righteous man" and whom God can address with the words "O man!" because it can be said of him that "his face was pure." But even this purity is not undisputed, whether in its love, its joy, its seriousness or its stillness. Even his aloneness by night with his star is disturbed, he is pursued, "his murderer sought him." So he falls, an innocent and pure man; the murderer overtakes him, his head sinks down. Yet of this head we are told: "Silver it fell, the head of the not-yet-born." Of the not-yet-born? He who could stride through the days and the years as a parable of the wholeness of life—unborn?

In the dark associations of Trakl's world, being born is identical with dying. The death of one phase is the birth of another. The child, the boy, the young man, Elis, Helian, the Caspar Hauser of an unborn life dies. He dies at the hands of the murderer who sees him, the shadow of the murderer,[45] the shadow of the Evil One,[46] which falls across him and which turns him into an evil man, a murderer and a wolf.[47] But this process of being overwhelmed by evil is identical with being born, with coming into "the world," entering the world of "grown-up" people, which is a cursed and a lost world because in it everything is lost that belongs to the world of Cas-

---

45. Ibid.   46. *Dichtungen*, p. 157.
47. Cf. "Aus goldenem Kelch," *Die Jugenddichtungen* (Gesammelte Werke, ii, Salzburg, 1939), p. 139. [Cited as vol. ii.]

par Hauser, of whom it could be said that "God spoke a gentle flame into his heart: O man!"

The birth of the world-ego with its ego-consciousness that belongs to the world of the day necessitates the death of the childish ego, which belongs essentially to a quite different world. That is why the childish ego reverts to a mythical ego, to which the world appears as a unitary world. It is in this realm that the childish ego and its world are integrated. Trakl's life and poetry are determined by the conflict between the world of the day and the nocturnal world and by the movement of withdrawal in which it becomes increasingly obvious that the poet is surrendering the "real" world of the world-ego and returning to the prehistoric world of the mythical ego. Why it should be that this return home is not simply a matter of regression and loss, but also involves a breakthrough to a comprehensive view of the reality of the world, will become clear in the course of our enquiry.

To be born involves a fall into the fate which is encountered by man at puberty and which is constellated by the world-ego and by the instinctual world associated with it. The world of the "unborn" is the life of innocence, as it was in the case of Caspar Hauser. Characteristically, however—though Trakl was not fully conscious of this fact—life in the Caspar Hauser Song is conceived as a life of imprisonment or containment in a sheltering and protecting environment. The emergence from this period of "unbornness" and of childlike innocence is accompanied by a corresponding change in the world, which had hitherto been perfect and undivided. Thus birth into the "grown-up" world and the overwhelming and overshadowing of the childlike world by the murderer are in fact identical, and the "evil" of the murderer appears as a symbol for the incursion of the overwhelming instinctual world of sexuality and for an aggression that has been driven to the point of destruction.

This explains an idea which is extremely significant for Trakl, the idea, that is, of the original sin of man, who is by nature essentially "fallen" and a member of an accursed race. However deep the connection may be between Trakl's own fate and this interpretation of existence, it is still essential to realize that here, as in all "great art," the personal and uniquely individual dimension is only a kind of introductory experience to the world of the transpersonal and the archetypally eternal that has taken shape in Trakl's poetry.

In Trakl's youthful drama *Bluebeard*,[48] the sadomasochistic element in sexuality and particularly the "first night" or "blood bride night"[49] finds expression in an extreme form. Here the traditional Bluebeard motif is enacted in an ecstatically bloodthirsty way, and though the youthful overemotionalism has a repellent effect, the play still has something grandiose and magnificent about it. The audacity of this ten-page, one-act puppet-play transcends the realms of both reality and fairy tale and finally achieves a mythical dimension; yet the very real shock and torment of the adolescent who is overwhelmed by sexuality shines through the immaturity of the form, and behind this we catch a glimpse of the total motive

48. "Blaubart," vol. II, p. 33.
49. Ibid., p. 34.

force of life experienced in terms of guilt. When Blue-beard calls out to the intoxicating moon of his own mania for blood:

> If things go round in circles, then
> Stand still for me, you drunken coracle!
> And get thee behind me, God-Satan![50]

he is formulating the background of moon, blood, in-toxication, and death that is familiar to us from the psychology of women, and in which the moon appears as the Lord of Blood and the Lord of Women, who deflowers them, impregnates them, and gives them both menstruation and intoxication.[51]

In this poem of Trakl's the association between evil, the murderer, and destruction can be traced back to its original source in mythology. An understanding of basic personal and transpersonal experiences, of actual incest and of the mythical Marriage of Death makes it possible to decipher many similar associations in the poet's per-sonal experiences and in his poetry.

With the Feminine, the interdependence between the onset of sexuality and the Marriage of Death is obvious enough. The fact that the bride "dies" when she gives herself up and surrenders to the bridegroom is an essen-tial part of her archetypal image.[52] The association of

---

50. Ibid., p. 40.

51. See my "Über den Mond und das matriarchale Bewusst-sein," II ("The Moon and Matriarchal Consciousness"), in *Zur Psychologie des Weiblichen* (Umkreisung der Mitte, II; Zurich, 1953).

52. See my *Amor and Psyche: The Psychic Development of the Feminine.*

blood with sexuality in menstruation, defloration, preg-
nancy, and childbirth is to be found at the heart of
woman's "blood mystery."[53] What happens now in
Trakl's case is at once unique and illuminating. He, the
representative of the masculine principle, is overwhelmed
by the same background of mythical and symbolic associations. Just as the masculine is experienced by the
feminine as the "death-bringer" in the Marriage of
Death, so it now experiences itself; that is to say, the
masculine in Trakl becomes "the murderer," and for this
the Bluebeard motif is the appropriate expression.[54] Here
man becomes not only a beast but a "beast of prey."
That is why the terrified bride cries:[55]

> God help me now! You slavering beast!

and Bluebeard replies:

> Call it a bull or an ape, as you may,
> Or another savage beast of prey!
> Ho! Lustily wooing the whole night through
> Till one beast alone is made out of two
> —And the name of that one beast is—Death!

Here the association, which is typical in Trakl's case,
between the symbols of evil, murderer, "red wolf," and
"hunter" and himself as the representative of the masculine principle is as clearly marked as is the association

53. See my *The Great Mother*.
54. In this context it is not possible to do more than mention
the association between "bluebeard" and the moon which is
actually found in mythology.
55. Vol. II, p. 43.

between the feminine principle and the dove, the victim, the game and the quarry. So Bluebeard says:

> Little child, if I'm to possess you all
> I must slit your throat—that is God's call—
> And suck out from you, deep inside,
> Your virgin's shame and your virgin's pride,
> You dove, and drink your red blood, your breath,
> Your quivering, foaming body's death.[56]

In still a similar vein we find the following passage in Trakl's late first prose poem, "Dream and Mental Darkness":

> In his fever he sat on the icy stairway, raging against God, asking to die. O, the grey countenance of horror when he raised his round eyes over the severed throat of a dove.[57]

The murderer is always "one possessed." That is exactly what is so horrifying about it. In his murderous assault he has himself been assaulted by the murderer or by the shadow of Evil, so that he is not only a murderer but also, invariably, at the same time a victim and a cripple.

> With icy hands, under naked oak trees, he strangled a wildcat. To the right, the white form of an angel appeared, mourning, and in the dark the shadow of the cripple grew. But he lifted a stone and flung it at the cripple, who fled howling, and the gentle countenance of the angel faded, sighing, in the shadow of the tree.[58]

56. Ibid., pp. 42-43.
57. "Traum und Umnachtung," *Dichtungen*, p. 157.
58. Ibid.

To be a murderer is the fate not only of man in the masculine sense of the word but also of human beings as the members of an accursed race; it is the fate of the "grown-up" human being as such. That is why to be born and to become a murderer is one and the same thing. The sadistically aggressive components of Trakl's sexuality and psyche are symbolic of man's condition as a creature at the mercy of Satan, the murderer seen as the Lord of this World, who rules in every human creature, but especially every masculine one.

It is one of Trakl's most deeply rooted characteristics that he is incapable of enduring this evil and masculine side of his nature. The feeling of guilt that pervades his whole work and tragically undermines his life, and the suffering inflicted on him by this evil element, which is of course by no means unconnected with his actual and symbolic rape of his sister, becomes in Trakl's case identical with his real feeling for life as such, and therefore with his basic mood of refusal or incapacity to live this life, in and as a state of guilt. He experiences his state of possession by evil as "alienation," and himself, the boy—Caspar Hauser in fact—as someone who, in the murder that has been committed, has himself also been murdered, so that, in the basic identity of murderer and murdered which is essential to Trakl's psychology, hunter and quarry, brother and sister merge, coalesce, and change places with one another.

Yet even this most intimately personal motif is also a universal human theme, since man, particularly in the masculine sense associated with the world-ego, that is, man who rapes and disfigures nature, not only destroys a

world and creates a bloody sacrifice, but is himself in the
process both raped and disfigured, so that the murderer
inside him is turned into a cripple. That is why life in
this denatured and raped world is an antechamber to
hell.

> In cool rooms, without meaning,
> Furniture rots, with bony hands
> Unholy childhood
> Fumbles in the blue for fairy tales,
> The plump rat gnaws cupboard and door,
> A heart
> Stiffens in snowy silence.
> Echoes resound in decaying darkness,
> The purple curses of hunger echoing,
> The dark sword-blades of lies,
> As if somewhere a brazen gate had slammed.[59]

As a part of this degenerate world we find a degenerate,
"unholy" childhood:

> Sometimes he remembered his childhood, filled as it
> was with sickness, terror and darkness, and of secret
> games in the starlit garden, or how he fed the rats in
> the twilit yard.[60]

But childhood, too, had many faces:

> On the way home he found an uninhabited castle. In
> the garden stood crumbling gods, mourning away over
> the evening. But to him it seemed: here have I lived
> forgotten years. An organ chorale filled him with holy
> awe of God.[61]

59. *Selected Poems*, pp. 83, 85 (C.M.).
60. *Dichtungen*, p. 155.   61. Ibid., pp. 155-56.

But apart from the forgotten years in the uninhabited castle there was another life, something deeper and more horrible, something "awful" that had nothing to do with the awe of God:

> But he spent his days in a dark cave, lied and stole and hid himself away, a flaming wolf, from the white countenance of the Mother. O! the hour when he sank down with stony mouth in the garden of the stars and the shadow of the murderer came upon him! With purple forehead he went out onto the moor and the wrath of God chastised his metallic shoulders; O! the birches in the storm, the dark beasts that shunned his benighted paths. Hate burnt up his heart, and lust, when in the verdant summer garden he did violence to the silent child and perceived in her radiant features his own shaded countenance. Woe! in the evening, at the window, when a glimmering skeleton, Death himself, stepped out of purple flowers. O! towers and bells! And the shades of the night fell like stones upon him.[62]

This poem is Trakl's own story and at the same time the story of mankind, Trakl's own childhood and the "unholy" childhood of modern man rolled into one. It is this unity of the mythical with a personal dimension which makes Trakl's poem great poetry. The unshelteredness of not being loved, which Trakl experienced in relation to his own mother, is characteristic not only of him but of the unshelteredness of our whole age, which has lost its connection with the maternal—with the ground root of the psyche. In Trakl, as so often, the search for the maternal takes the form of an addiction—an attempt to return to the mythical Great Mother.

62. Ibid.

The repudiating, negative side of the Mother appears
not only in his terror of "the white countenance of the
Mother" but also in the form of the "Terrible Mother,"
the "Plague Mother." That is why we are told in the
second poem of the cycle entitled "The Accursed":[63]

At evening hems the Plague her robe of blue
And a dark visitant softly shuts the door.
The maple's black weight through the window falls;
A boy lays down his forehead on her hand.
Often her eyelids droop, evil and hard.
The young child slips his fingers through her hair
And his tears gush out quickly, hot and clear
Into her black and empty eyehole pits.
A nest of scarlet-coloured serpents rears
And lazy writhes upon her livid thigh.
The arms release the little body—dead.
The sadness of a carpet enfolds it.

What a mythical grandeur there is about this Plague
Mother and Plague Goddess and how horribly alive is
the motif of "nobody loved him" in the symbol of "not-
being-looked-at," the fearsome opposite to "finding grace
in her eyes"! What a pinnacle of desolation is expressed
in the image of the child vainly stroking his mother's
hair and of his tears gushing out "into her black and
empty eyehole pits"! That the deepest level of the archetypal image of the Terrible Mother has been evoked
here is confirmed by the fact that her flesh, as always in
the experience of mankind,[64] is associated with deadly

63. Ibid., "Die Verfluchten," pp. 117-18.
64. See my *The Great Mother*, p. 153, etc.

serpents, which actually bring about the death of the child.

It makes no difference whether the "child" in fact perishes at the hands of the murderer or as a result of the embrace of the Plague Mother, the blue Indian goddess Kali. The murderer is an inseparable companion of the Plague Mother in her role as the Terrible World Mother;[65] action in this context is always murderous action.

We know about Trakl's desperate hate-love relationship with his mother. She is one of the basic facts of his existence. Both his flight to the love of his sister and his passionate yearning for the embrace of the nocturnal Mother are dominated by the dark fatality of this relationship. There is scarcely any other passage in poetry in which we find the connection between the negative primal relationship to the mother and the collapse of the child into sickness and evil so briefly and monumentally formulated as in the prose poem "Dream and Mental Darkness":

> Nobody loved him. In twilit rooms, lying and unchastity burnt up his head. The blue rustle of a woman's robe petrified him to a pillar, and in the doorway stood the nocturnal figure of his mother. Above him rose the shadow of Evil.[66]

The unlovingness of the stony mother turns her into a Gorgon who "petrifies" her victim. Over and over in Trakl's poetry we find the hostility to life of this "stony"

65. See my *The Origins and History of Consciousness.*
66. *Dichtungen*, p. 157.

quality, which appears as something accursed but not actually dead. So we read, still within the boundaries of the human realm, that "under the suffering hands of the Mother, the bread became stone,"[67] and, leaving the human realm behind us:

> Under dark fir trees
> Two wolves mingled their blood
> In stony embrace.[68]

For the same reason hell is called "stony,"[69] and so are the slaughtering shades of the night.[70]

In her role as the Terrible Mother, the mother leads and misleads the child into evil, yet at the same time she is the admonishing figure of the everlasting reproach, who breeds anxiety in the child, petrifies him, and by petrifying him drives him further into evil or alternatively into flight from evil and ruin by addiction. So the "petrified countenance of the Mother"[71] weighs on the boy in the form of the "curse of the degenerate sex":

> But he spent his days in a dark cave, lied and stole and hid himself away, a flaming wolf, from the white countenance of the Mother.[72]

> Swaying, a shape of lamentation,
> The mother moves through the lonely wood
> Of this speechless grief,[73]

67. Ibid., p. 161.   68. Ibid., p. 143.   69. Ibid., p. 191.
70. Ibid., p. 156.   71. Ibid., p. 155.   72. Ibid., p. 156.
73. *MGP*, p. 133 (D.L.). [The abbr. = *Modern German Poetry 1910–1960, An Anthology* . . . , ed. Michael Hamburger and Christopher Middleton (London and New York, 1962). The translator's initials are given.]

but the intoxication of poison is also subject to her spell:

> Deep is his slumber under dark poisons, filled with stars and the white countenance of the Mother, the stony one.[74]

His deepest feeling of guilt is connected with the figure of the Mother, who as Plague Mother represents ruin, as mother of addiction, intoxication, as unloving mother, evil, and as complaining mother, despair at existence in a state of evil. It is the indescribable quality of this mother-image, which in its unlovingness towards the child as a person transcends all personal considerations, that makes it so unspeakably terrible. But this same transcendent quality makes it inexorable, and it fills the world. Everywhere the accursed man is cursed to encounter the dark Mother who repudiates encounter. Whether he flees from her into the evil of real action or withdraws into intoxication to avoid this evil—nowhere can he evade the empty gaze of her deadly countenance.

In the words "the appearance of the Mother in pain and horror,"[75] the personal and the suprapersonal, archetypal qualities of this Mother are combined. The poet's poetical imagination comprehends something that belongs to this world—something real—whose validity is eternal and whose image appears everywhere and always in human history, but what makes Trakl's poetry peculiarly the poetry of our own time is that this something is stirred into animation in the most uncanny way by the horror and the need which is the specific experience of modern man in the West. The insecurity of contemporary existence threatens all childhood today, since it casts its shadow over the mothers themselves, who are and represent security and shelteredness for the child. Just as in the poet himself a universal human dimension surrounds what is uniquely and individually human, so his own childhood is every human childhood and his flight from the world and his personal ruin are symbols of a peril that threatens humanity at large. The personal merges into the transpersonal, the individual into the collective, Trakl's own mother into the World Mother, his own childhood into the morning of mankind, his own mental darkness into the darkness of our time, his own downfall into the death of the West:

> Gruesome sunset red
> is breeding fear
> in the thunder clouds.
> You dying peoples!
> Pallid billow
> that breaks on the beaches of Night,
> stars that are falling.[76]

In its dreamlike and symbolic intermingling this mutual coalescence of personal and transpersonal is by no means confined to the figure of the "Mother."

So we read in the second section of "Revelation and Downfall":[77]

Silent I sat in a deserted tavern under smoke-blackened roofbeams—alone, over wine; a radiant corpse bent over a dark thing—and at my feet lay a dead lamb. Out of

76. *MGP*, p. 139 (M.H.).
77. "Offenbarung und Untergang," *Dichtungen*, p. 191.

putrifying blueness stepped the pale figure of the sister
and thus spake her bleeding mouth: Prick, black thorn!

Unquestionably the allusion here is to the dark happening, the sexual symbolism of which is almost entirely
undisguised. The end of the same section,[78] "And gently
the blood ran out of the sister's silver wound and a fiery
rain fell upon me" belongs to the same context. But the
figure of the sister as a victim merges imperceptibly into
that of the lamb. And when we read in another passage,
"So that he should never forget his fate and the thorny
sting,"[79] it is clear that the symbolism has shifted, and
in "thorn" and "sting" fate and desire become the
scourge of existence itself, as the poet says in another
passage:[80]

> Under arches of thorns,
> O my brother, blind minute-hands,
> We climb towards midnight.

So too the symbol of the sister as a victim and as a child
reechoes in the symbolism of another context. The sentence "So he found in a thorn-bush the white figure of
the child, red with blood from the mantle of her bridegroom"[81] is associated with the image of the "dead
lamb," and behind all this appears "the black head of
the Savior in the thorn-shrub."[82] It is only in the light
of this context that it is possible to understand the
strange words addressed to the sister in the first of the
Rosary Songs, which is entitled "To My Sister."[83]

78. Ibid.   79. Ibid., p. 159.
80. *Selected Poems*, p. 69 (M.H.).
81. *Dichtungen*, p. 159.   82. Ibid., p. 79.
83. *Selected Poems*, p. 17 (D.L.).

O Good Friday's child, at night stars seek
Your forehead's curve.

The association of the sister with the Crucified might
appear at first sight like blasphemy, and it must in fact
remain so for any Catholicizing interpretation of Trakl.
Yet in spite of isolated Catholic elements, Trakl's poetry
is derived from a far deeper, more uncanny layer of the
soul that is not domiciled in any specific culture. Corresponding to the curse laid on the aggressive and de-
structive masculine principle, which is seen as the murderer, the wolf, and Bluebeard, there is a bleeding feminine principle, which is depicted as suffering, sacrificed
and pursued by the hunter, and in the mythical world
of the West the hunter is very often associated with the
Satanic, killing principle.[84] The sister, whom Trakl personally loved and in relation to whom the drama of his
fate was enacted, always continues to be included in the
meaning, yet as victim and quarry she has a wider significance, since she represents the soul itself, whose
destiny of suffering in the world is fulfilled by her. This
means that the subject of the poem is not Trakl's soul
or any *one* soul in particular, but the destiny of the human soul itself or of the world-soul.

It is not simply that the poetry always reaches out be-

84. This layer, in which the hunter represents the "evil masculine principle," is matriarchal from the psychological viewpoint.
When development thrusts its way forward to the dominance of
the patriarchate, the accents change in a characteristic fashion.
Then we find—for example, in the fairy tale of Little Red Rid-
inghood and in the "Seven Little Kids"—that the wolf is identified with the "Evil Mother" but that the hunter now plays the
part of the liberating masculine principle.

GEORG TRAKL

yond the personal into a transpersonal dimension, but
that the meaning of this outward-reaching movement
becomes clear at the very moment when it breaks
through into an experience and a shaping into symbolic
form of the unitary reality, which is now no longer
identical with "this" world, as conceived in terms of the
"nothing-but" world of the daylight ego. The coincidence of the "personal" and the "transpersonal" that
takes place when Trakl is no longer writing poetry as
a person, but when the poetry inside him becomes a
song, is identical with the overwhelming of his world-
ego by the mythical ego; and this is the central problem
of his life and work.

The "gentle madness"[85] that grew stronger and
stronger within him finds expression both in the increasingly mythical trend of his poetry and in the rapid
advance of his mental illness, which culminated in his
final downfall. Intoxication, dream, and mental derangement reach a unique accord in Trakl's poetry, but the
yearning for a deeper and more sheltered reality finally
overwhelms him in the form of a craving to escape from
the hostile, alien world of normal reality.[86] His life and
work as a poet run their course along an exceedingly
narrow path, on the brink of a downfall into madness
and death—into which they finally collapse.

With the emergence of the mythical dimension in
Trakl's poetry, all the plastic elements relating to this

85. *Dichtungen*, p. 54 inter alia.
86. The compulsive notion that he would be shot as a deserter,
which resulted in his death, belongs to the same context. Cf.
Spoerri, p. 29.

181

world fuse into a unity that nevertheless gives the impression not simply of a dream but of the shaping of a deeper and "other" reality. In many ways the music of the poems, with its strange rhythm, follows the techniques of self-expression which are employed by the unconscious and which we have learned to understand in the interpretation of dreams. His poems are alive with fusions, displacements, and identifications, expressed in a picture language of symbolic significance that conveys to us the world of the prelogical, with its dissolutions and nonconceptual plastic forms. And yet this poetry remains real even when it approaches the limits of our understanding or actually moves in the realm of the incomprehensible, and it enchants us with the fascination of a unitary world that infinitely surpasses the comprehension of our conscious minds at the very point where it grips us and moves us most deeply. Just as in dreams figures emerge, encounter, and part from one another, which may seem immensely strange and alien to us, but which may still be parts of our own strange and alien inner world, so in Trakl's poetry figures appear and reappear that we can understand both as parts of his own psychic world and at the same time as independent figures in a dreamlike, poetic, and superpersonal dimension of the psyche.

Although we know that Trakl did not write his poetry in a state of somnambulistic unconsciousness but as a consciously creative and formative artist who was concerned to improve his poetic material and to seek out an adequate form of expression for it, the fact remains that this somnambulistic, dreamlike quality is an essential characteristic of his poetic output. Trakl's vision of the world as a single reality that is located in a dimension beyond inner and outer finds expression in the way in which the living and the dead, external and internal, reality come and go without distinction or demarcation in his poetry. So we read at the end of the "Song of the Hours":[87]

Sweeter smell yellowed fruits; gentle is the laughter
Of the happy one, music and dancing in shady cellars;
In the twilit garden step and stillness of the departed boy.

We take it as a matter of course that in all poetry figures which appear "objectively" as persons are at the same time inner figures in the imagination of the poet, so that, for example, Faust and Mephistopheles, for all their appearance of worldliness and externality, also represent two aspects of Goethe's psyche. This is true of all lyric poetry, and it applies all the more to Trakl's case, since in his work the quality of inwardness is so marked and the "figures" that appear in it belong so obviously to this inner world. As the power which creates poetry in Trakl grows stronger and the figure of his conscious world-ego recedes in favor of the mythical ego, the psychic realm broadens out into a world of poetry in which the poet is included as one actor in the drama— very much like the ego of the dreamer in a dream. But this actor lives—again as in dreams—in the closest and most intensive relationship with the world which is unfolding and with the other figures which make up that world. The fluctuating character of this interdependence

87. "Stundenliedes," *Dichtungen*, p. 99.

arises out of the fact that the relationship between the ego that is writing the poems and the poetical world that we have described is a relationship both of identity and of nonidentity, and each of these *two aspects is* emphasized in turn. The figure of the "murderer," like that of the "boy," exists both as an endopsychic figure in Trakl and as a transpersonal reality, which contains and at the same time transcends the figure of the shadow or of the childhood ego that belongs to the inner being of the poet.

Heidegger is therefore wrong in principle when he asserts that "Elis is not a figure which Trakl intends as a representation of himself. Elis is as essentially different from the poet as the figure of Zarathustra is different from Nietzsche."[88] In the first place, the question that is answered here is not posed correctly. The poet does not "intend" that a certain figure should represent himself. He is that figure without intending it, and whether he knows it or not depends on the kind of poet he is and on the extent of his knowledge of himself and of the relationship between his work and his life. "Not to intend" can mean either *to be unconscious of* this actual relationship or to be aware of the limits of this relationship. When Faust cries "Two souls, alas! reside within my breast,"[89] Goethe is undoubtedly aware that in the persons of Faust and Mephistopheles this duality has become incarnate in two actors in the drama; yet the autonomy of the psyche which creates the poetry and

88. Martin Heidegger, "Georg Trakl. Eine Erörterung seines Gedichts" (a discussion of a poem), *Merkur*, vii:3 (1953), p. 238.
89. *Faust*, part i, scene ii, tr. by Bayard Taylor.

the process by means of which its component members achieve independence in a poetical world transcends any intention on the part of the poet to represent himself or indeed any intention of the poet at all. How often in Trakl's poetry "the boy" stands for the eternal innocence of humanity and of the masculine sex! And yet, when we read, in "Sebastian in Dream":[90]

> So dark was the day of the year, desolate childhood,
> When softly the boy to cool waters, to silver fishes
>   walked down,
> Calm and countenance;
> When stony he cast himself down where black
>   horses raced,
> In the gray of the night his star possessed him

—who could fail to see that this was Trakl's own childhood? Who could forget the child who threw himself in front of the bolting horses and walked into the water and was only rescued because his hat floated above him on the surface of the pond?

Quite apart from the question as to whether the poet does or does not identify himself with a figure in his poetry, the double relationship of being and at the same time being other than applies in any case. This declaration of independence by the poetic psyche, in which the ego no longer governs the creative process but at best makes some contribution to the poetic happening, is the "gentle madness" which is involved in poetry of any kind, but particularly in lyrical poetry. When the poet reaches this condition of being "outside himself," of

90. *MGP*, p. 121 (M.H.).

"enthusiasm," of "being in the realm of the divine," he transcends existence in the normal outside world and enters a greater and different reality, in which the power of madness, in the sense of "holy madness," that dissolves familiar situations and connections and creates new ones, is the ruling principle.

In Trakl's poetry the frequent association of the word "madness" with the epithets "gentle" and "soft"[91] points to a dissolution of the hard crust of the daylight world, in which the unrelated, segregated, and lonely aspect of things and people appears in the sharp demarcation and differentiation of the light of the conscious mind. But the gentle world of madness is the world of the moon, of blueness, and of night, in which different colors, sounds, and aspects of reality shine out. In Trakl's case, the process of withdrawal from the daylight world and of turning towards this other, nocturnal form of reality often takes place under the influence of the "poisons" of wine and of "the poppy"; the drunkenness caused by these agents numbs the consciousness of the daylight world and allows the world of "mental darkness" to emerge. Surrender to this world is Trakl's deepest addiction and yearning, and his poetry is the expression of this surrender.

> O how dark this night is. A purple flame
> Failed at my mouth. In the stillness
> The alarmed soul's lonely music fades and dies.
> Let be, when the wine-drunk head sinks down
> to the gutter.[92]

91. *Dichtungen*, pp. 33, 54-55.
92. *Selected Poems*, p. 45 (C.M.), slightly altered.

In this "let be," all "letting-go-of-the-world," all "letting-yourself-surrender" and all "letting-yourself-be" is included. And whether it is a case of "your eyelids are heavy with the poppy" or "drunk with the poppy," this drunkenness is always the drunkenness of the night, of euphony and of poetry. So we hear in the poem entitled "Ecstasy":[93]

> Silently dwells
> Upon your mouth the autumn moon,
> Dark song drunken from poppy juice,

or at the end of the "Seven Songs of Death":[94]

> On a darkling boat he was carried down
>   glimmering waters,
> Clustered with purple stars, and peaceful
> Sank down upon him the fresh green branches,
> Poppy from silver cloud.

But the deadly peril of real madness and real downfall threatens, close at hand:

> Cursed be you dark poisons,
> White sleep![95]

or:

> Deep is his slumber under dark poisons,
> filled with stars and the white
> countenance of the Mother, the stony one.[96]

93. "Verklärung," *Dichtungen*, p. 141.
94. "Siebengesang des Todes," ibid., p. 139.
95. Ibid., p. 178.   96. Ibid., p. 160.

The deadliness of sleep and death is here mingled with the deadliness of the maternal, and the poem sings tragically, in a thinly veiled, uncanny accusation:

> Mother bore this infant in the white moon,
> In the nut-tree's shade, in the ancient elder's,
> Drunk with the poppy's juice, the thrush's lament.[97]

In Trakl's poetry the embrace of the night is the dark redemption which is his only hope of escape from perdition in guilt and putrefaction.

> O the putrefied figure of man: jointed
>   together from cold metals,
> Night and the terror of sunken forests
> And the scorching wilderness of the beast;
> Windless calm of the soul.[98]

When the ego is submerged in drunkenness this dark amalgam is dissolved, man's face disintegrates, unfeeling metallic substance achieves independence, night and the terror of sunken forests come to life, and the scorching wilderness of the beast springs wolfishly at man, but in the windless calm of the soul the nocturnal boat stands motionless in its own reflection. Only the song itself is redemption in the form of drunkenness, which is and becomes a song in which the destiny of man unfolds as a world.

In the process of withdrawal the world-ego darkens and is deranged, and in poetic form the world of the unitary reality achieves color, sound, and shape. But as the ego is dissolved and reemerges as a world, some-

97. *Selected Poems*, p. 47 (M.H.).
98. *Dichtungen*, p. 138.

GEORG TRAKL

thing quite different is also happening, that is to say, a
resumption of the relationship with the dead and departed guiltless existence, which nevertheless continues
to live as an element in psychic life.

The original innocent wealth and abundance of the
reality of the day has long ago been disfigured by guilt,
accursedness, and putrefaction; yet this daylight reality
is encompassed at its beginning and ending by the
deeper reality of the nocturnal, in which the not-yet-
born and the unborn, that which has passed away and
that which is dead, find their place together in a world
apart. The innocence of this domain extends into the
life of every single human child in the shape of the primeval world of mankind. It is only gradually that the
child grows up into the guilt-laden world as we know
it, so that it may achieve there its second birth, disfigured though this is by original sin. It is for this reason
that when we leave childhood behind us we are saying
goodbye to our own unbornness. The figures of "Elis"
and of "the boy" are symbols of this existence that still
lives on in the original state of peace and innocence.

> Or the footsteps of Elis
> Ring through the grove
> The hyacinthine
> To fade again under oaks.
> O the shape of that boy
> Formed out of crystal tears,
> Nocturnal shadows.[99]

or:

99. *MGP*, p. 137 (M.H.).

The dark shape that came from the coolness still
   follows the wanderer
Over the footbridge of bone, and the boy's hyacinth voice
Softly reciting the forest's forgotten legend,
And more gently, a sick thing now, the brother's wild
   lament.[100]

In contrast to the scorching redness of wolfish lust, the
boy is associated with coolness. With his hyacinthine
voice he belongs to the blue realm and follows the
wanderer, the guiltily lost world-ego, on the bony footbridge of death. As so often in Trakl, the "forgotten
legend of the forest" is "what has been forgotten," that
is to say, the memory of the world of innocence. For
the adult who has become guilty, the boy is "moldered,"
yet he lives eternally in the blue realm of the world
apart, the wholeness of a real existence in the beyond,
which encompasses the unborn, the dead, and the living.
"In the twilit garden, step and stillness of the dead
boy."[101]

So we read in "Helian":

Let the song also remember the boy,
His madness, and white temples and his departing,
The moldered boy, who opens bluish his eyes.
O how sorrowful is this meeting again.[102]

The fate of the boy is summarized in these lines. He becomes mad in the negative, murderous form of being
overwhelmed by evil; his temples become white:

100. *Selected Poems*, p. 57 (D.L.).
101. *Dichtungen*, p. 99.
102. *Selected Poems*, p. 31 (C.M.).

And leprosy grew silver on his forehead.[103]

Silver glisten the evil flowers of the blood on his brow.[104]

The dead boy, his hyacinthine voice, and his shadow—
this is the radiantly eternal part of a reality, the sunken
self of a childhood, which the man who has become a
wanderer and a stranger has lost. But this state of being
abandoned by one's own purity and authenticity is alienation at the deepest level. It makes a man a stranger
and results in an unauthentic existence, the loss of a
man's "countenance" and the kind of despair that drives
a man to suicide. And yet this despair and the madness
of the guilty man represent at the same time a renewal
of the encounter with the figure of innocence and its
righteousness. Yet even this grace of encounter is for-
feited when the evil deed in its unrepentant brutality
violates the cripple, the man's own deformity and the
righteousness of the angel himself, whose presence is
revealed by the sound of his sighing and then disappears:

> To the right, the white form of an angel appeared,
> mourning, and in the dark the shadow of the cripple
> grew. But he lifted a stone and flung it at the cripple,
> who fled howling, and the gentle countenance of the
> angel faded, sighing, in the shadow of the tree.[105]

Here the white figure of the angel almost merges into
the figure of the boy, who even in the depths of guilt-

103. *Dichtungen*, p. 159.   104. Ibid., p. 160.
105. Ibid., p. 157.

laden despair shines out like a source of comfort, which can never be lost.

> But as I descended the rocky path, madness seized hold of me and I cried out aloud in the night; and as with silvery fingers I leaned over the silent waters, I saw that my countenance had forsaken me. And the white voice spoke to me: Kill yourself! Sighing, a boy's shadow rose up in me and looked at me with radiant eyes, till I sank down weeping under the trees, under the mighty vault of the stars.[106]

Anything which we might say here would be inadequate to capture what the poet's mythical ego could express by his art in the hymn "To the Boy Elis" and the poem "To One Who Died Young." The figure of "Elis," the "one who died young," transcends all personal experience. Already in the figure of the boy the greater figure of the angel and "eternal boy" could be glimpsed as a divine presence; in the figure of Elis this presence emerges more distinctly from the indefinable obscurity of the background and lives as a "mystical friend" in and near the deranged poet. When we read:[107]

> Elis, when the ouzel calls in the black wood,
> This is your own decline.

and:

> O Elis, how long you have been dead,

this in no way contradicts the following verses, which belong to the same poem:

106. Ibid., p. 192.
107. *Selected Poems*, p. 35 (M.H.).

But you walk with soft footsteps into the night,
Which is laden with purple grapes,
And move your arms more beautifully in the blue.

In the poem "To One Who Died Young,"[108] he is a "gentle playmate in the evening"; we are told, it is true:

But the other descended the stone steps of the
Mönchsberg,
A blue smile on his face, and strangely ensheathed
In his quieter childhood, and died.

Yet in spite of this, the one who survived and who came out into the evil of the world had the experience that the "ghost of the one who died young quietly appeared there in the room," and

In a lonely room
Often you ask the dead child to visit you,
You walk and talk together under elms by
the green riverside.[109]

This dead-and-living quality of Elis is, in its tender, juvenile beauty, a masculine form of the psychic element that fills the world, just as the sister is the feminine form of this world-soul. The poet's love, sunken into itself and deranged as it is, belongs to this youthful friend, who not only walks beside him as a dead boy, but also meets him in the transformed world, wherever that world is "absolute" or perfect:

Absolute is the stillness of this golden day.
Under old oak trees,
Elis, you appear, one resting with round eyes.[110]

108. Ibid., p. 71 (C.M.).   109. Ibid., p. 73, slightly altered.
110. *Selected Poems*, p. 37 (M.H.).

And when the poet sings:

Oh how righteous, Elis, are all your days,

then it is the righteous world, the right world of stillness
to which he is appealing, the world that is always lost
when the stranger is wandering around in the world of
alienation.

Since Elis is poured out like a cascade throughout the
whole of nature, wherever nature has remained divine,
the poet can sing:

A gentle chiming of bells resounds in Elis' breast
At nightfall,
When to the black pillow his head sinks down.[111]

But at the deepest level of the poetic vision Elis becomes
the center and heart of the night, the theophany of the
nocturnal moon-god:

A golden boat
Sways, Elis, your heart against a lonely sky.[112]

Just as the semidivine or divine figure of Elis lives in
the personal-impersonal psyche of the poet in the figure
of the boy, the youth, the friend, the lost self, and just
as the mother, transcending the personal realm, coalesces
with the great figure of the nocturnal Mother, the same
kind of transformation applies in principle to the image
of the sister, the central figure of Trakl's existence.

If we are to understand Trakl's personal fate, we must
start from the loneliness of his motherless childhood and
the deadly way in which he was exposed to a state of

111. Ibid.   112. Ibid.

abandonment that was unconsoled by any primal relationship with the mother. The absence of or a disturbance in this basic relationship to the mother is the most frequent cause of mental illness and addiction; however, this loss is almost always countered by a helpful intervention on the part of the psyche, which seeks to restore the balance by activating the archetypal image of the Mother in the unconscious. This activation of the image of the Great Mother is in fact a characteristic feature of the work of a large number of creative artists, including, for example, practically all the Romantics. The Great Mother, who unites in a single image the good and the terrible mother, may appear as a positive vision of the Beyond in the form of a greater, calming reality; however, the impact of a negative world in the here and now may seem so overwhelming to the little ego that in its feeling of helplessness it may yearn for an all-embracing protector, and this yearning may turn into a longing for death and a passionate desire for an escape from the world and for a self-extinction in which this downfall will be experienced as the supreme ecstasy of a death in love.[113]

Very often this archetype of the Great Mother appears positively in mystical and emotional experiences of "nature" or landscape, which is experienced as an all-embracing, calming, and dissolving reality. Traditionally this "matriarchal" existence is everywhere associated with the symbols of night and of the moon; that is why, for example, in early civilizations (most of which were

113. See my *The Origins and History of Consciousness*, index, s.v. incest, uroboric.

originally matriarchal) the reckoning of time almost invariably starts with the evening.

In Trakl's poetry, too, evening, the blue of twilight and night are seen as times and seasons of life itself, which is experienced as the day and the year of the soul. The lost early years of childhood innocence correspond to morning and springtime, and the reality of an existence from which both the sick man and the poet in Trakl fled corresponds to the world of midday. But in the evening, the autumn of the day which belongs to the last things, the "real" and great world, the world of night, begins, and it is from this world that the darkly glowing colors and sounds of Trakl's poetry and the enchantment of his brightly colored addictions are derived. This nocturnal dominion of the blue, of the Night-Mother, is the time of mental darkness, of gentle madness, and of the intoxicated slumber in which the ego goes down, while the other, visionary, mythical ego that creates the poetry comes into view.

Such an overwhelming power on the part of the Great Mother, which appears psychologically in the form of an overmastering superiority of the archetypal, mythical, archaic world, is invariably associated with an immature ego that has not achieved its complete masculinity—with a "youthful," juvenile ego, in fact. The tragic conflicts that are played out between the "Great Mother" and her "youthful son," his impotence in relation to her, his vain resistance to incest with the Mother, his attempts to liberate himself as a "struggler" in the secret society of the males, and his final downfall in addiction, madness, and self-destruction are—both in myth and in the psychic reality of mankind—typical expressions of the inferiority of the masculine vis-à-vis the matriarchal.[114]

In the normal development of a boy, as of a girl, the child's primal relationship with the mother and his attachment to her comes first and foremost, in every sense. She is his most decisive experience of the "feminine," and this remains true even when, as a result of the son's necessary detachment from the mother, her image recedes into the background of the psyche. The image of the mother, which was originally overwhelming and omnipotent, must normally fade and be replaced by the figure of the feminine in its capacity as the sexual partner and the "you" of an adult human relationship. At the same time the masculine ego develops and grows out of a passive and childlike attitude towards the maternal into the active and adult posture that is required for the conquest of the sexual partner and the subsequent position of the man as the father of the family.[115] This development normally begins in early days, when the child is still quite small. It is at this stage that the image of the feminine in the form of the sister, the playmate and companion, makes its appearance. In her, the boy meets a you of the same kind as himself but of the opposite sex, and his relationship to this you provides a vehicle for a whole host of developments that are essential for the maturation and self-discovery of the masculine and its liberation from the overmastering superiority of the maternal image of the feminine. This "separating-

114. Ibid., index, s.v. "Strugglers."

115. See my "Die Angst vor dem Weiblichen," in *Die Angst* (Studien aus dem C. G. Jung Institut, xii; Zurich, 1959).

out" of the feminine as a comrade from the feminine as the superior maternal principle is a process that begins in childhood and only reaches its conclusion in and after puberty, when owing to the injection of adult genital sexuality the image of the sister is overlaid and replaced by the image of the woman, who is now also the sexual partner and the complete, all-round companion.

Although sexual factors also play a part in the boy's relationship with his sister, these are not the decisive consideration, since it is in the latency period that the sister succeeds the mother as the dominant image of the feminine, and this period comes to an end with the onset of puberty. It is not until then that the asexual figure of the sister is overlaid by or coalesces with the figure of the sexual partner. This means that the characteristics of the sister figure are in their essential nature "sisterly": the sexual characteristics are not stressed. Apollo and Artemis are archetypal prototypes of this constellation, in which the feminine is asexual or even hostile to sexuality, because the psychic and sisterly characteristics are predominant. It is for this reason that in the psychology of the male the sister is always associated with the virginal as a type of the "higher feminine."[116] There is an opposition between the aphrodisiac side of sexuality and this aspect of the feminine, which in the case of mental illness may result in a split in the masculine capacity for love, so that the two aspects do not combine but exclude one another.

However, this "normative" development is an optimum condition, and there are numerous disturbances

116. See my The Great Mother.

and defective and incomplete developments that run their course side by side with the norm. For example, the mother-image may still be dominant in the image of the partner and the development of the "sisterly you" may be lacking or insufficiently emphatic; on the other hand, there may be an overvaluation of the sisterly component, and this may result in a negative evaluation of the sexual partner and a split between the sexual partner and the "sister"—or the emphasis on the sisterly component may be so strong that a relationship with a sexual partner becomes simply impossible. This means that both the mother-fixation and the sister-fixation have to be overcome if the male is to achieve a maturity that will make possible an adult relationship with a woman which will include sexuality. On the other hand, a successful relationship with the figures of both mother and sister is necessary before the male can enjoy an adult relation of partnership with a woman.[117]

The question of the psychological necessity of the incest taboo inevitably arises at this point and some answer to this question must be attempted. The very fact that this taboo is practically the only law which is common to all known human societies suggests that it is vital to the development of the human race. The obvious validity of the incest taboo can be explained if it is derived from the fact that the male is required to develop his symbolic and actual masculinity through the vehicle of his relationship with his mother and his sister, since these—or other relatives who correspond to them—are the first

117. *Mutatis mutandis*, corresponding conditions apply to a woman's relationship with her father and brother.

female objects of his nascent capacity for man-woman relationships.

It has been said, perhaps with justice, that it is vital from a genetic standpoint that man should range widely and interbreed with other groups because in this way he can achieve more favorable genetic combinations, whereas inbreeding in obedience to the tendency towards incest will inevitably result in an accumulation of pathological genes, which can only have a damaging effect. Yet apart from this doubtful biological situation, there is an incontestable psychic advantage. Both mother and sister correspond to transpersonal archetypal "images" in the psyche, which are triggered off by the boy's actual relationship with his own mother and sister and in the process absorb some personal characteristics from these "real" figures. At the same time, however, they retain a character of "universality" that transcends all personal considerations. The mother represents the Great Mother[118] and the sister the "soul-image" (a part of the anima[119]), and as such they are essential components or qualities within the masculine psyche. Normally the overcoming of the tendency to incest with the personal figures of mother and sister results in a reinforcement of the endo-psychic figures, which are then projected onto the outside world, where they initiate and reinforce the outward movement of the young man's libido and his relationship to the world and to women outside the family circle.[120]

118. See my *The Great Mother*.
119. See my *The Origins and History of Consciousness*.
120. Cf. C. G. Jung, "The Psychology of the Transference," CW 16.

Thus the Great Mother is activated as a figure of the unconscious and is projected onto the whole fabric of the world, whether this takes the form of nature, home environment, country, social grouping, etc. This means, however, that both for the individual and the collective, the opportunity to make this vital projection and attachment depends on the fact that incest with the mother has not actually been committed and that the mother in her archetypal form has not been sought and found in the immediate family circle but in the broad compass of life in the world. It is for this reason that the prime concern of all primitive initiation rites is the overcoming of the drive to incest with the mother and the successful projection of the mother archetype on the outside world.

In the psychic development and economy of Western man, the figure of the "sister," the overcoming of the tendency to incest with her, and the projection of the anima-image which is associated with the sister play an equally important part.[121] In the figure of the sister the feminine does not appear primarily as a sexual partner— let alone a sexual object—but as the "You" who is different by nature and who, for this very reason, possesses the "psychic" quality that is associated with the soul-image. The emotional and intuitive side of the feminine, which in the conscious mind of the "normal" male is not so strongly developed, is appreciated by him as a "soul,"

121. In other cultures different but analogous developments occur. In cases where the ban on incest is so absolute that the sister and the characteristics which she represents do not come into contact with the brother at all, this vital component for a mature man-woman relationship is necessarily lacking.

an inspirer, a "feminine spirit."[122] Owing to the repression of the incestuous attachment to the sister, this unconscious soul-image is activated in the psyche of the man and in this way becomes ready for projection, so that it can be projected outwards on the feminine principle and can help to determine the man's relationship to it.

This means that the repression of the real tendency to incest with the sister results in a differentiation of the masculine psyche, which is of vital significance and importance for the choice of the marriage partner and the creation of a human family. The marriage of modern Western man, which is our principle concern in this context, presupposes this activation of the "anima" of the husband.[123] This implies that when the male becomes fully mature as a result of the affirmation of the incest taboo, the qualities represented by the sister are introjected and in this way associated with the fully developed inner image of the feminine partner. But since the sister, and not the beloved woman in her role as the sexual partner, represents the "psychic" element and can only be reached by psychic means, the taboo on incest with the sister remains genuine.

122. See my *Zur Psychologie des Weiblichen* and *The Great Mother*.

123. A large proportion of modern marital conflicts arise from the fact that this anima-projection does not—except perhaps for a brief period—provide a viable basis for the subsequent maturation of an integral relationship. However, this question, and the problems that affect women in a corresponding psychological situation, cannot be dealt with here. Cf. the problem of the "integral relationship" in my "Die Angst vor dem Weiblichen."

On the other hand, if the male has not arrived at the stage at which the image of the sister is associated with the beloved woman and if he is unconsciously only looking for a "sister" in marriage, then either the woman he has married will be reduced to "a mere woman" (in which case the man's anima-side will remain unfulfilled and he will look for other "sisters"), or else (as often happens when the marriage partner is identified with the mother) the man will be impotent.

In general, civilization tends towards a "normal development," which in our context implies a strict adherence to the incest taboo. The cultural canon and its collective representatives appear in the form of the "world" and the "social environment," which persuade the individual to achieve an adjustment to the requirements expected of him and in fact compel him to a large extent to sacrifice his wholeness as expressed in his creative individuality. The "automorphism" of the individual,[124] his inborn tendency to unfold as a unique, creative personality, involves him from his early childhood in a conflict with the cultural requirements of his society, and his relationship with "himself" and with the unconscious as the creative part of the individual psyche has to be surrendered in favor of his relationship to the world and the social environment.

In the case of the creative artist, however, automorphism and the inner compulsion to develop as an indi-

124. See my "Narcissism, Normal Self-Formation, and the Primal Relation to the Mother," tr. Hildegard Nagel, *Spring* (New York), 1966 (orig. 1955).

vidual remain the dominant influence, irrespective of whether this comes about as a result of fate, constitutional factors, or a combination of the two.

This psychic situation of the creative artist that deviates from the "normal development" also finds expression in a change in the relationship to mother and sister. In the artist the tendency to incest with both these figures is not repressed in the "normal" way but in a certain sense continues to exist, though this is not a matter of a "sexual," but of a total psychic condition of relatedness, in which the sexual factor is included but is not the decisive consideration.[125] In one of his books,[126] Otto Rank has collected and interpreted from the psychoanalytical standpoint a wealth of material, on the basis of which he has demonstrated, particularly in the case of poets, the overwhelming conscious—and still more unconscious—importance of incest with the mother or sister. Among creative artists—and by no means exclusively poets—a "psychic" relationship with the "sisterly" form of the feminine plays a leading part as a source of inspiration and in the form of "Sophia."[127] This manifestation of the feminine stripped of all its earthly qualities is beloved by the male creative artist, and the exalted anima-figures of these relationships—Beatrice and Laura, Frau von Stein and Beethoven's "immortal beloved"—all, both in their "unapproachableness" and in their understanding

125. See my *The Origins and History of Consciousness*.

126. *Das Inzest-Motiv in Sage und Dichtung* (Leipzig and Vienna, 1912).

127. This is not to say that the corresponding feminine "counter-figures" of the "negative" anima—the seductress, the prostitute, the vamp, etc.—do not also play a decisive role.

and redeeming "otherness," possess the essential characteristics of the sisterly.

In the creative artist the anima-side of the sister is the image of his own, unconsciously reinforced psychic quality and creativity, and its influence is so powerful that it cannot entirely be repressed. It is in fact projected for this very reason, yet characteristically the relationships that arise in this way are by preference "distant loves," which must not be irritated by the proximity of sexuality or of "real" living together. So Goethe, for example, loves a whole series of "sister-anima" figures— yet he marries the unsisterly Christiane. That is why the interior character of the sister-anima in her capacity as a "soul-image" is so often directly opposed to the externality of any possible sexual partner. As with every archetype, the reality of the sisterly is the living image not only of part of the outside world—in this case of the feminine part—but also of the subject's own unconscious psychic structure. The sister-soul corresponds to the inspiring psychic quality of the creative masculine psyche, and its dominant influence corresponds to an overemphasis on psychic productivity which vies with the concrete human relationship, since the artist's relation to the inner world as a universal human dimension takes precedence over his relationship with the individual human being.[128]

128. If the creative artist is an extravert, the same process takes place, the only difference being that in his case the universal human dimension has a worldly rather than a psychic character; in his case, too, the "creative task" is more strongly emphasized than the human relationship, or at least rivals it in significance.

In a certain sense the creative artist—unlike the normal man—never entirely "loses" his soul to a woman, since she always remains creatively alive within him in the form of an inner authority. This predominance of the typical sisterly qualities in the character of the man's anima means that the psychic life of the creative artist, his relationship to the unconscious and beyond that to the unitary reality, never leaves him entirely free. It does not follow that the creative artist is incapable of developing a mature partnership relation. However, even when such a relation exists, his relationship to the "soul," to his inner productivity, retains its predominance and vies with his relation to the human "You." But when this anima-image is projected onto a real woman, the resultant "anima-love," especially if it is love at a distance, will be marked by an exceptional intensity. Such a distant relationship is not likely to be disturbed by many elements deriving from external reality; it can expand with greater energy and freedom in the form of a psychic reality, and in this way approach nearer to the archetypal. That is why Dante's "real" Beatrice is comparatively unimportant—like the "reality" of Beethoven's "immortal beloved." On the contrary, the paler and more "distant" the beloved is, the easier it is to ascribe to her that quality of redeeming and inspiring understanding which is expected of her as the "soul-sister."

The activation of the mother and the sister archetypes, which means in this context the failure to overcome the

See my "Leonardo da Vinci and the Mother Archetype," in *Art and the Creative Unconscious.*

tendency to incest, is always associated with a predominance of the unconscious. In cases where there is mental illness this makes a normal development and the corresponding adaptation to the environment and the ruling cultural canon impossible. In the case of the creative artist we find the same preponderance of the archetypes and an analogous difficulty in achieving a normal development and adaptation. However, when we call a man creative as opposed to pathological, we are thinking of a person who, in spite of this unusual psychological constellation and in spite of his difficulties in making a "collective" adaptation to the world, produces an achievement or a work that is an expression of his own self-realization and is at the same time significant for the human species as a whole. It is a matter of indifference whether the contemporary representatives of the cultural canon either fail to grasp or deny the significance of a work of this kind.

In the by no means uncommon cases in which pathology and creativity go hand in hand and are in fact interdependent, it is impossible to determine, except by individual analysis, which psychic components should be regarded as pathological and which as creative. In the creative artist the transpersonal-mythical dimension is dominant, and the personal realm takes the form of a place where the impersonal dimension can be concentrated. This means that in every personal event the "archetypal resonance" always remains alive. The basic archetypal figures of the human psyche, which achieve realization and clear expression in the single and unique psyche of the creative artist, always shine through the events of the personal realm that are superimposed upon them.[129]

In Trakl's case, the fateful personal situation in which he was involved by the incest that did not remain a fantasy seems at first sight completely to confirm the psychoanalytical interpretation. In reality, however, it forces us all the more to extend the range of our interpretation, since we must not only include the transpersonal dimension of the event in its interaction with the personal realm, but must make this the center of our enquiry. As this is not a case of repressed instinctive feelings or of unconscious desires still awaiting discovery, the figure of the "sister" gains a new significance for the life and poetry of Trakl.

We have already drawn attention to the abrupt personality change that Trakl underwent at the onset of puberty. The incursion of evil, incest, "birth into the world," and the development of addictions all fall within this period of upheaval. Trakl broke down at the crisis of puberty, the dangerous transition from childhood to the world of adult life and of society, which in the world of primitive man is for this very reason safeguarded by initiation rites. When an average man suffers from a crisis of this kind the result is either a collapse of his personality and of the world as experienced by him, or a withdrawal from it into a drug-addict's world of artificial paradises. However, in the case of Trakl's inherently creative personality, something quite different occurs, namely the sudden emergence of his poetry, in

129. See the essays in the projected volume, *The Place of Creation.*

which the conflict between the artistic formulation of a primordial, essentially "other" world and of the unattainable and rejected "reality" of the adult world is thrashed out.

We must try to understand the meaning that "enacted incest" must have had for the development of Trakl's personality. Where there is incest between brother and sister, is this really anything more than the violation of a part of a cultural canon which is dangerous for everyone who belongs to this particular culture but not necessarily for every human being? As we know, guilt feelings are dependent on the super-ego, the conscience in the psyche of the individual, and the contents of this conscience vary with the cultural canon of the society concerned. The kings of ancient Egypt and of the Incas who lived in incest with their sisters could do so without the slightest psychic danger, since in their case marriage with a sister was recognized by the cultural canon. However, the meaning of the incest taboo, and particularly of the taboo against incest with a sister, goes deeper. It is, as we said, a "genuine" taboo; the "sisterly" quality represents something that is "intrinsically inviolable" in the human psyche. When—as in the case of the queens we mentioned—a particular culture lifts the taboo on the real sister, then the personal sister is reduced to the status of an ordinary woman, a possible marriage partner, who, in addition to other characteristics, may possess some sisterly traits.

"The sisterly" in its pure and archetypal form will then appear in the figure of the sacral virgin, the inviolable, virginal priestess, who embodies the archetype of the sister, and violation of the taboo on this sacral virgin is almost invariably punishable with death. In this context, we may recall the uncanny fact that both Trakl and his sister terminated their lives by committing suicide.[130] What, then, we must ask ourselves, is the nature of the psychic catastrophe that took place here? For, without question, it is the psychic reaction to "the deed" which is the decisive factor.

It is not sufficient to point out either that, in the loneliness of Trakl's childhood, his sister was for him the natural partner in love—just as he, the big brother, was for her, or that, for the youth, the sister whom he glorified was "the most beautiful girl, the greatest artist, and the strangest woman" he had known.[131] Her significance extends far beyond these extremely important personal factors.

In contrast to the "accursed world" of the adults, childhood is for Trakl the representative of a suprareal and primordial world of purity, which is in its essential nature inviolate and inviolable. But above this world shines the double constellation of the brother and sister in the pristine innocence and beauty of a companionship for which "Elis" and "the sister" are the characteristic figures. The brother and sister are a pair unstained by any taint of evil, and as such they are the symbol of an inviolable unity that lives in the realm of the divine. It is the double unity of a sacred marriage, that is to say of a supremely exalted and integral incest, which partici-

---

130. The question as to whether Trakl's death was a half-unconscious suicide does not alter this fact.

131. Spoerri, p. 39.

pates in the nature of eternity. The sacred unity of the intimate connection between brother and sister is a living embodiment of the inviolability of an archetypal image of the self, in which the unity of masculine and feminine is preserved and safeguarded.

It is the image of the divine primordial man, of whom the Bible speaks in the Book of Genesis: "So God created man in his own image, in the image of God created he him; male and female created he them."[132]

This divine double unity of the primordial man, this symbol of the self, was experienced in the childhood love of the brother and sister as a supreme, unquestioned, still and holy reality. The sacredness of the connection between brother and sister is based on the living archetype incarnate within it, which represents the unity of the bisexual self in the form of the unity of brother and sister. This unity is extramundane and preindividual, its field of action is the pure realm of a still incompletely differentiated childhood, in which something boyish is still alive in the girl and something girlish in the boy. In this double unity masculine and feminine are preserved and related to one another in their true essential nature, without yet being involved in the "opposition" between the sexes from which the tension of sexuality derives its power. In the life of their transpersonal brother-and-sister relationship, which has not yet been disrupted by ego-consciousness, inner and outer, I and You are still one. That is why the sister is both within and without: she lives as sister in their childhood home and, at the same time, in the blue realm of the psyche. But this

132. Genesis 1:27.

211

means that if Trakl violates her in any way, he is also violating himself, his own psyche and the reality in which both he and she have their real existence. It is in these terms that we should understand the two-in-one unity of brother and sister, which still shines through, even in the later stages of Trakl's decline, as we can see from the following passage: "When in the verdant summer garden he did violence to the silent child and perceived in her radiant features his own shaded countenance."[133] And "Woe to the stony eyes of the sister, when at the meal her madness entered the brother's gloomy forehead."[134]

In the course of normal development it is necessary that this unity of a divine existence should be lost and replaced by the mundane polarization of man and woman, whose union in marriage not only guarantees by its fertility the continuance of the human race, but also procures the alliance of two contrasting individualities in a supraordinate unity which forms the sacred nucleus of family, social grouping, community, and culture.

Normal development involves to a large extent the surrender of creativity in favor of a recognition of generally accepted cultural values and the sacrifice of individuality to an adjustment to the requirements of the collective. In point of fact, the normal development that is appropriate to the first half of life is determined far more by the claims of society than of the individual; yet the survival and the creative endurance of this sacrifice provides the indispensable basis for the individuation process of

133. *Dichtungen*, p. 156.   134. Ibid., p. 161.

the second half of life, which is world-embracing in the true sense of the word, as it includes the whole range of man's world experience. Thus the young male's entry into the development of the first half of life, which takes place under the dominant influence of the world and the collective, is associated with loss and sacrifice, with the surrender of life in the archetypal world, in the unitary reality and in childhood, and this also involves giving up mother and sister and losing the world that they represent in the interior of the psyche.

And here we are confronted with one of the tragic problems of human existence, with which mankind comes to grips in its religions, its philosophies—and its diseases. The archetypal world of childhood which has to be surrendered is divine, but the world that the adolescent now enters is an earthly, human, cruel world which is profoundly contaminated with evil. That is the reason why life in this world is interpreted as the "fall" of man and as "sinful," and his "original" and "earlier" state as a condition of pristine innocence. This negative interpretation corresponds to certain basic human experiences, and the plethora of crises and diseases which erupt at puberty or begin during that period all revolve around the same central problem of man's participation in an innocent, or alternatively in a guilty, world.

Man is generally enabled to negotiate this transition by means of the "initiation rites," which are used by society to compel the individual to surrender his individual existence and to experience himself as a responsible and transpersonal member of the equally transpersonal community, which is regarded as being in communion with the world of the ancestors. This means that the relationship of the growing adolescent to the community is the essential prerequisite for the process of initiation, which enables him to surmount the crisis of puberty and to become an adult male.

The basis of the human capacity for relationship is the primal relationship with the mother. A successful primal relationship makes the child capable of love and of mutual relationships, but it also develops in him a capacity to live his own life in spite of everything, or in other words to adapt himself as an automorphous personality to the environment and at the same time to hold his own and to expand as a unique individual. An unsatisfactory primal relationship leads to a negative overstressing of the mother archetype, which endangers not only the child's capacity for love and community but also the normal development of the ego. This results in a pathological reinforcement and narrowing of the ego in the form of an "emergency ego"; alternatively, the weakened ego, which is not strong enough to defend itself and the world of its conscious mind, is in constant danger of being overwhelmed by the contents of the unconscious.[135]

One essential difference between the sick person and the creative artist in cases where there has been a disturbance in the primal relationship with consequent accentuation of the mother-archetype is that in the cre-

135. See my "Narcissism . . ." The significance of the matriarchal phase for the psychology of childhood will be demonstrated in another paper.

GEORG TRAKL

ative artist this nearly always leads to a powerful reinforcement of ego-development, which in conjunction
with the activation of the unconscious by the mother-
archetype results in a heightening of tension. It is from
this tension that the creative achievement finally
emerges.[136]

There can be no doubt that in Trakl's case—quite
apart from his quality as a creative artist—there was a
basic disturbance in his primal relationship with his
stony mother. Both his own picture of the "stony"
mother and the objective information we possess about
her—her unrelatedness, dissatisfaction, proneness to addiction, and lack of interest in the children—are evidence
of her failure, which is one of the main causes of Trakl's
severely damaged capacity for relationship. His almost
compulsive attachment to his sister is no proof of the
contrary. Everything we are told about him supports
the conclusion that he lacked any genuine capacity for
relationship with human beings. The impact that he
undoubtedly made upon people and his violent fits of
affection for animals do not really alter the position.
There was no real friend and—apart from his sister—
not one single loved or loving woman who played any
significant part in his life. Even the people who were
most friendly towards him and who admired him as a
poet and loved him as a tragic human being could make
no really close contact with him.[137]

This profound lack of relationship in Trakl which was

136. See my essay "Man and Transformation," in *Art and the
Creative Unconscious.*
137. Cf. Spoerri on this point.

215

caused by the disturbance in his primal relationship with his mother resulted in a reinforcement of his deep roots in the primeval and pristine world of childhood and the colorful abundance of its archetypal symbolism. Together, these two factors made the advance in development to the "adult" level of normal man that is required of the adolescent male at puberty completely impossible in Trakl's case. It is this which enables us to understand the catastrophic impact on Trakl's life and work of the incest with his sister which occurred during this period. When the sacred pristine brother-sister relationship is invaded by sexuality this world of purity in a divine existence degenerates. Evil is triumphant, the twin constellation of brother and sister is shattered, the boy is "murdered" and perishes, the youth is "born" into a world that is accursed by evil, and by violating his sister he violates himself and makes himself a cripple and a murderer. So the incest in his life is the "fall of man"; it is analogous to the gnostic myth of the intrinsically pure soul which originates in the upper world but is attracted by the lower world and by evil and falls into the power of Satan, the Lord of this World.

Trakl's yearning and addiction now takes the form of an attempt to withdraw from this world; by the use of drugs he tries to find his way to the world that is dead and gone, the world apart. Yet this withdrawal, which is at the same time derangement and downfall, leads—and that is the greatness of Trakl's poetry and the proof of his creative genius—not only to regression and decay but also to rebirth and transfiguration.

In "normal life," too, the deserted world of childhood and the symbols of the archetypal world and the self that emerge during this period are not simply lost, although this may seem to be the case at first. The constellations which glowed in the sky of childhood are the same as those which appear above the horizon once again in the second half of life and in the process of individuation, the process, that is, in which the individual becomes himself. In Trakl's last great poems, as often happens with creative geniuses who die young,[138] the original starry world of childhood and its subsequent return are both given a form in which the soul, now enriched by the fullness of life, is reflected with greater clarity and magnificence than in the springtime of their earlier inviolability. The bridge to this earlier world apart, and also to the world that emerges later on, is provided by the figure of "the sister." In her image, which contains both beginning and ending, the sister invariably combines doubles and opposites: she is love and death, youth and maiden, nearest and furthest, "flaming daemon"[139] and "woman stranger"[140] at one and the same time. Yet here, as so often in Trakl, one thing mingles "gently" with another, since when the poet experiences himself as "the stranger," the "woman stranger" is his nearest neighbor in the community of strangeness.

In "The Soul's Springtime"[141] Trakl can sing:

138. See my "Zu Mozarts Zauberflöte" ("On Mozart's Magic Flute"), in *Zur Psychologie der Weiblichen* (Umkreisung der Mitte, II).

139. *Dichtungen*, p. 158.   140. Ibid., p. 190.

141. *Selected Poems*, p. 97 (D.L.).

O my sister, when I found you by the lonely clearing
In the wood, at noon, in a great silence of all animals,
You were white under the wild oak, and the silver
    thorn-bush blossomed.
A mighty dying, and the singing flame in the heart,

Yet he can also lament:

Again his forehead darkens by the moonlit rocks;
A radiant youth
The sister appears in autumn and black putrefaction.[142]

However varied the forms may be in which the sister appears, she is essentially an apparition of evening and the night. This mingling of the sister with the great images of the nocturnal is first suggested when we read:

Sister, your blue eyebrows
Gently beckon in the night.[143]

But her fusion with the mythical realm of night and mental darkness is unmistakable in the verses that describe the poet's downfall:[144]

The blueness of my eyes was extinguished in this night,
The red gold of my heart. O! how still the light burned!
Your blue cloak embraced the sinking one;
Your red mouth sealed the mental darkness of your friend.

The sister, who is seen here as blueness and evening, melts into a mythical darkness, in which the light of the sun sinks to rest, just as the world of the moon and the stellar luminaries emerges out of it. In the poem

142. *Dichtungen*, p. 108.　　　143. Ibid., p. 188.
144. Ibid., "Nachts," p. 98.

entitled "Evening Song,"[145] it becomes clear to us in the most wonderful way how the sister unites in her own person beginning and ending, spring and autumn:

> In the evening, when we walk on dark paths,
> Our pallid images appear in front of us.
> When we are thirsty,
> We drink the white waters of the tarn,
> The sweetness of our sorrowful childhood.
> We have passed away and we rest under elder bushes,
> And gaze at the gray gulls.
> Spring clouds climb over the dark city,
> Which holds the nobler days of the monks in its silence.
> When I took your slender hands,
> You gently opened your round eyes.
> That was long ago.
> Yet when dark euphony visits the soul,
> You appear, a white form, in the autumn landscape of
>   your friend.

In the line "Yet when dark euphony visits the soul," the word "visitation" touches many chords of color and tone. The "dark euphony" of the poem and of the world which sings in mental darkness is received by the soul, and that is what "visits" it. When the twilight draws in and the soul that has been visited is fulfilled, the world of the tired traveler inclines towards its end; it grows "autumnal," and it is now a friend to the stranger. But the sister becomes like the Hebrew "levanah," the White One; she becomes the shining one, the feminine "moon." Just as "Elis" in his boylike divinity becomes the moon, so the sister now becomes the divine image of shining

145. Ibid., p. 81.

unity, which was represented in earliest childhood by the now long-lost double unity of brother and sister. As Trakl's poetry merges into the mythical realm, the sister becomes the nocturnal feminine principle and the moon, to which mythology has so often ascribed an image that is both masculine and feminine and at the same time sexless.

In this masculine-feminine moonlike quality of the sister, the unity of brother and sister vibrates as an interchangeable I and Thou, inner and outer.

The poetic prose of "Dream and Mental Darkness"[146] is still under the spell of the fatal act:

> A purple cloud darkened his head, so that silent he fell upon his own blood and his own likeness, a moonlike countenance; stony, he sank down into the void, when in a broken mirror, a dying youth, his sister appeared; night swallowed the accursed generation.

Another poem[147] merges into the mythical:

> O brazen ages
> Buried there in the sunset red.
> From the house's dark hall there stepped
> The golden shape
> Of the maiden-youth
> Surrounded with pale moons
> Of autumnal courtliness.

In her role as the moon the sister is inseparably connected with the blue realm and the darkness of the nocturnal:

146. Ibid., p. 161.   147. *MGP*, p. 141 (M.H.).

Where you walk, there it is autumn and evening,
A blue deer under trees and its music,
A lonely pond in the evening.[148]

When she appears and then disappears in the darkness,
the sister- and mother-archetype merge into each other,
but the sisterly quality never becomes devastatingly terrible; even when it means the dark embrace and the
downfall, it is never corruption.

When the "cloistress" is invoked as darkness:

"Cloistress! Close me in your darkness,[149]

she still always remains the sister of the monk, of the
one who is departing, the lonely one who is a stranger
in the world. The title of the poem that begins with this
verse is in fact "Surrender to the Night." Just as the
stranger has his counterpart in the woman stranger and
the youth in the maiden, so the monk has his counterpart, not in the nun, a word with a different derivation,
but in the sisterly "cloistress" [German *Mönchin*[150]].
This is one of Trakl's most profound and remarkable
inspirations. Behind it gleams the word "Ischah"
(woman), the feminine form of the Hebrew "Isch"
(man), which was translated by Luther as "Männin"
for this reason. It is not for nothing that monks and
cloistresses [*Mönchinnen*] are also known as brothers
and sisters.

148. *Selected Poems*, p. 17 (D.L.).
149. *Dichtungen*, p. 189.
150. [This word was coined by Trakl; the literal English
equivalent is "she-monk." This, however, does not express the
moonlike quality suggested by the original.—Tr.]

> Autumn night, so cool, advances—
> Sparkling with stars
> Over shattered bones of men:
> The quiet moon-cloistress.[151]

The masculine and the burning passion and clamor of sex are alike overcome in the sexlessness of monasticism. Fall and twilight are associated with the end of the world of blueness, the transfigured existence of the nocturnal and the feminine.

When the moonlike, luminous quality of the sister is darkened, everything becomes estranged and shrinks back into negativity:

> Cloud obscures the moon. Blackish fall
> By night from the tree wild fruits;
> Space becomes a grave,
> This earthly pilgrimage a dream.[152]

This "dream" is something deathlike and black; it is not the dreamlike transfiguration of the blue, which is Trakl's color for the world of the unitary reality. Even when, in the poem entitled "Lament,"[153] "eternity's icy wave" is invoked, it is the face not of God, of Christ, or of "Man," but of the sister which shines above these verses, almost the last that he wrote, the verses which portray his final downfall:

> Sister of stormy sadness,
> Look, a timorous boat goes down

151. *Selected Poems*, p. 113 (R.G.), amended.
152. *Dichtungen*, p. 189.
153. *Selected Poems*, p. 119 (M.H.).

222

Under stars,
The silent face of the night.

Even under the silent face of the night she is still his comforter.

Yet although this sinking of the boat may represent the actual termination of bodily existence in the same way that the mysteriously obscure death of the twenty-seven-year-old poet was the end of his physical life, the limit of possible experience does not in fact coincide with the end of life, any more than the process of disappearing into the abyss is identical with the nadir of blackness in Trakl's poetry. The poet's entry into the blue realm is a homecoming, a return to the world, which is both downfall and origin. At first sight it may still seem as if there is a darkening of the gold of experience here—as if it is a case of "Melancholy,"[154] in fact.

> Again and again you return, Melancholy,
> O gentle sadness of the lonely soul.
> A golden day burns to its close.
> In humility the patient one bows to the pain,
> Resonant with euphony and tender madness.
> Look! The twilight is already falling.
> Night returns and something mortal laments
> And another shares its suffering.
> Shuddering beneath the autumnal stars
> Each year the head sinks down lower.

But the derangement, the gentle madness, is revealed more and more clearly in its essential nature as the

154. "In ein altes Stammbuch" ("In an Old Album"), *Dichtungen*, p. 55.

drunkenness of the mystery, the celebration of a mythical incest, an entry into the maternal and sisterly domain of the night.

The mythical incest with the realm of the nocturnal is, however, not simply derangement—in many mysteries narcotics and ecstasy open this doorway into the darkness—but this incest is also an entry into the blue realm of the world apart. The reconciliation with fate and the transfiguration of everything that has life takes place in a region of the world-soul in which the human dimension is changed back into something naturelike, animallike and creaturely in spirit.

> For always there is a blue deer following,
> A blue deer eyeing under twilit trees,
> Following these darker paths,
> Wakeful and stirred by nocturnal harmony,
> Gentle madness.[155]

When the poet, in another passage,[156] referring to this region of the world-soul, exclaims, "O this dwelling in the quickened blueness of the night," it becomes clear to us that this "night" is something essentially different from the noctural as contrasted with its opposite, the day. This world, since it is the world of a mystery, is a "spiritual" world. In the experience of the unitary reality, the spiritual coalesces with the psychic and the reality of the world to form a single, unitary whole. The real is now a symbol and the symbolic is real and belongs to the world. In the mystery of this experience, what is

155. *Dichtungen*, p. 143.
156. "Gesang des Abgeschiedenen" ("Song of the Departed One"), *Dichtungen*, p. 174.

mythical becomes human and what is human and fateful becomes a myth; yet in both these dimensions the "spiritual" existence of man and the world becomes transparent.

> Quiet on the edge of the forest is found
> A dark deer;
> On the hill the evening wind drops gently,
> The blackbird's lament grows dumb,
> And the soft flutes of the autumn
> Are silent in the sedge.
> On a black cloud
> You cross, poppy-drunk,
> The nocturnal tarn,
> The starry sky.
> For ever the sister's lunar voice
> Sounds through the spiritual night.[157]

This is the experience of the mystery in which, as in a myth, the Great Feminine is revealed as a unity of upper and lower, of starry sky and "nocturnal tarn."[158] The intimate entwinement of what is real in this world, of forest and deer, blackbird and sedge, starry tarn and the lunar voice of the sister, with the gentle madness of the spiritual experience is transfigured and becomes a poem.[159]

In the mystery, when the worldly ego is replaced by the mythical ego:

157. *Dichtungen*, p. 135.
158. See my *The Great Mother*.
159. See my "Die Erfahrung der Einheitswirklichkeit" ("The Experience of the Unitary Reality"), *Eranos-Jahrbuch*, xxiv (1955), p. 59.

On a dark cloud
You cross, poppy-drunk,
The nocturnal tarn,
The starry sky,

then the "transfiguration"[160] is achieved, of which the
poet sings:

Silently dwells
Upon your mouth the autumn moon,
Dark song drunken from poppy juice.

In its "mental darkness" the mythical ego of the poet
appears as a "moon-ego"; it is a "lunatic"[161] in every
sense of the term and its fate is a lunar fate. It is bound
to the realm of the nocturnal; in the world of the sun
it is a stranger, and it is extinguished by that world. Its
light shines out in the "twilight" and the "evening,"
when the blue region of the world-soul begins its reign,
and it is in this region that its own rising and setting
are enacted. The moon-ego is a wanderer, and as a wanderer it is a stranger. It is only in a state of drunkenness
that this stranger links up with the blue realm of the
sister and—far in the background—with the darkness of
the mother. The wanderer can only find rest in his setting, he can only "dwell" as one who is declining and
afflicted with mental darkness. It is his voc-ation to be
the voice of the nocturnal.

In the mythical incest of this mystery, existence becomes meaningful as "Revelation and Downfall," as the

160. *Dichtungen*, p. 141.
161. See my "Über den Mond und das matriarchale Bewusst-
sein" ("The Moon and Matriarchal Consciousness"), in *Zur
Psychologie des Weiblichen* (Umkreisung der Mitte, II).

nocturnal song of the world which is the world-soul.
In it, the ego is taken up once more, in the form of the
mythical ego, into the "Beyond," into the blue realm,
and there, "risen again," it becomes a unity, "One kin,"
with the archetype of the sister.

> O! the bitter hour of decline
> When we regard a stony face in black waters.
> But radiant the lovers raise their silver eyelids:
> *One* kin. From rosy pillows incense pours
> And the sweet canticle of the bodies resurrected.[162]

In this union, the *hieros gamos* of the sexless state of
"identity-with-each-other," the extramundane self of the
brother-and-sister hermaphrodite is realized. As the consciousness of the "transfiguration" emerges and dies
away again, the curse of fate is lifted,

> When the grandson in his mind's gentle night,
> Lonely, ponders the darker ending,
> The quiet god closes his blue eyelids over him.[163]

The entry into the blue realm and the acceptance
("let be!") of drunkenness and gentle madness dissolve
the stoniness of the evil which threatens every human
being from the world of the ancestors, who take possession of his blood. But in the suffering and transfiguration of the grandson and in the "beauty of a generation
which is returning home,"[164] the emphasis shifts from
sin and from the world which is accursed to the greater
unitary reality which embraces them.

162. *Selected Poems*, p. 77 (C.M.).
163. Ibid., p. 33 (C.M.).   164. *Dichtungen*, p. 190.

... and from eyes dark with night
The brother quietly gazes at you,
That he may rest from his thorny wanderings.
O this dwelling in the quickened blueness of the night.
Lovingly too the silence in the room embraces the
    shadows of the ancient ones,
The purple tortures, lament of a great generation,
Which now dies devoutly in the lonely grandson.
For ever more radiant from the black minutes of madness
Awakens the suffering one on the petrified threshold
And there surround him mightily the cool blueness and
    the glowing decay of the autumn,
The quiet house and the legends of the forest,
Measure and law and the lunar paths of the departed.[165]

The world of the departed is the world of the transfigured, and their paths, the redeemed and redeeming paths, are "lunar." "Measure and law and the lunar paths of the departed": the radiant awakening is a radiant awakening into the "quickened blueness of the night," it is the transformation into Elis, the boy with the "lunar eyes,"[166] the divine moon, of whom the poet sings:

A golden boat
Sways, Elis, your heart against a lonely sky.[167]

In the mysteries of the Great Night-Mother, regeneration takes the form of rebirth as a star, and the infinity of the nocturnal starry sky is a reflection of the immortality which the "spiritual" Mother of the living be-

165. Ibid., pp. 174-75.
166. Selected Poems, p. 35 (M.H.).   167. Ibid., p. 37.

stows.[168] Through its transformation into the moon, the poet's ego is united with the feminine moon, who is the sister. But in the mystery of this transformation an even greater depth is plumbed, since the moon is at the same time the son-lover of the nocturnal Mother-Goddess. In him, the shining one, the Moon-Son, the writer of mythical poetry, the night itself is illuminated and the darkness of the nocturnal is transformed into sound. The same principle applies in fact to the poet of "dark madness" as to the *Magic Flute*:[169] the silence of the night is transformed into a voice.

On the "black walls" of the accursed cities "God's lonely wind"[170] is heard, and "the putrified figure of man" is bound up with the "windless calm of the soul,"[171] but at the end of "The Soul's Springtime"[172] we read:

Softly the waters murmur in the declining afternoon.
On the river bank the green wilderness darkens, the
    rosy wind rejoices;
A brother's gentle song on the evening hill.

So the world itself murmurs out of the stillness in the song of the poet of the night, of which the poet as a boy had already movingly and prophetically spoken:

168. See my *The Great Mother*.
169. See my "Zu Mozarts Zauberflöte" ("On Mozart's Magic Flute"), in *Zur Psychologie des Weiblichen* (Umkreisung der Mitte, ıı).
170. *Selected Poems*, p. 39 (M.H.).
171. *Dichtungen*, p. 138.
172. *Selected Poems*, pp. 95, 97 (D.L.).

I am the harp in your embrace;
Now wrestling for my life's last pain,
Sings in my heart your dark refrain
And makes me eternal, substanceless.[173]

In this final transformation into the mythical realm of poetry everything living becomes gentle, and it is out of this gentleness, out of the stillness and silence of the nocturnal, and out of the world of the blue that the voice now begins to sound:[174]

> Dark mouth, you are mighty
> Within, figure formed
> Out of autumn clouds,
> Golden evening stillness.

The dark mouth at the heart of the golden evening stillness is the power that sings in the poet, but it is also the voice of the blackbird and the sedge, the wind of God, which in the evening wind, in the "dark flute of autumn" and in the lunar voice of the sister becomes the sound of the soul, the music of poetry, and the "euphony of the poet's spiritual years."[175] So the poet himself becomes the dark mouth at the heart of the golden evening stillness, which redeems itself as a creator of poetry.

The poet's entry into the transfiguration of the nocturnal is his homecoming out of this world and its evil into the world apart of the unlost wholeness in the unity of the real.

173. "Aus goldenem Kelch," *Die Jugenddichtungen*, p. 60.
174. *Selected Poems*, p. 113 (R.G.), amended.
175. *Dichtungen*, p. 167.

When I went into the twilit garden, and the black
figure of Evil had departed from me, I was enfolded by
the hyacinthine stillness of the night; and I glided in
a curved boat over the tranquil tarn, and sweet peace
touched my stony brow. Speechless I lay beneath the
ancient willows and the blue sky was high above me
and full of stars; and as I gazed upon it and died, fear
and the deepest of my pains died within me; and the
blue shadow of the boy arose, radiant in the darkness,
a gentle song; there arose, too, on lunar wings over the
verdant treetops and the crystalline rocks the countenance of the Sister.[176]

176. Ibid., p. 193.

IV

FREUD AND THE FATHER IMAGE

To write a eulogy of Freud to mark the centenary of
his birth would be a totally superfluous undertaking,
since both the acknowledgment accorded to his work
and the effect it has had on the whole of Western civilization are unparalleled. Seldom have the obstacles that
are of necessity placed in the way of a pathfinder been
so quickly and completely overcome as in this case.
Freud has become the classic representative of depth
psychology barely fifty years from the time when he
himself was quite unheard of and when hardly anyone
knew the meaning of the word "psychoanalysis." The
outstanding success of Freud's work, which has transformed modern man's conception of life, is as much the
result of the absolutely unique and original quality of
his basic discoveries and of the brilliance of his prose as
of the fact that from him a new science was born.

Before Freud's time psychology had found expression
in the works of the great poets but, scientifically speaking, had remained a mere stepchild of philosophy. With

---

"Freud und das Vaterbild," *Merkur* (Stuttgart), no. 102 (May
1956).

Freud it burst into the consciousness of his time and was revealed as the fundamental science of the nature of man. We have before us, without always being aware of it, a remarkable phenomenon. Not only has everything previously called psychology been completely changed by this stepchild of philosophy, which is not a true science even today, but further, our entire knowledge of the nature of human health and sickness has been shaken and transformed by the assault of depth psychology on our conception of the world. Not only psychiatry and medicine but philosophy, the history of art, and that of literature; not only criminology but ethnology and sociology, have all been profoundly influenced by depth psychology. Our knowledge not only of the illnesses of mankind but also of those of the child and of primitive man, of the artist and of the criminal, has changed so fundamentally within the last fifty years that the ordinary person's approach to human nature—both the good and the evil sides of it—simply cannot be compared with the attitudes toward, the insights into, or the valuations of human nature held in the Victorian age in which Freud was brought up.

The biography of Freud[1] shows in a most illuminating way what an extraordinary personality he was. It also reveals the heroic efforts he had to make against his own psychic troubles in order to penetrate into the depths of the psyche. He attempted to bring into con-

1. Ernest Jones, *Sigmund Freud: Life and Work* (New York and London, 1953-57), 3 vols. [As the editions are differently paginated, U.S. and U.K. page references are given, respectively.]

sciousness and to formulate the results of the insight which he had gained, from working not only on patients but also on himself.

This new psychology bursts upon us from all the bookshops of the world, from professional books and journals, from scientific and semiscientific pocket editions, from novels and poems; it both enlightens and confuses us in the theater and at the cinema; in more and more new varieties of tests it tries to grasp and to pin down the essential nature of man; yet it is still in reality completely overshadowed by the great personalities from whom it emerged and is still emerging.

It is curious that the generation of pupils who are now trying to develop a scholarly science from these beginnings should overlook the fact that we are still living in the "heroic age" of psychology, in which the personalities of the founders, in all their greatness and smallness, must necessarily influence what they can express about the nature of man. This statement doesn't mean that we are joining those people who are, by their opposition to modern psychology, out of touch with their time. Nor should we underestimate the large number of psychologists all over the world who have done more or less valid scientific research. Nevertheless, one should bear in mind the extent to which depth psychology is still in its infancy and how tentative its interpretations must inevitably still be. The dogmatic certainty shown by many of its representatives demonstrates the fundamental insecurity of people who have not achieved enough inner stability to be able to afford a skepticism about all human achievement that may well prove fruitful.

Such a dogmatic attitude is in direct contrast to that of the "founders." In spite of their tenacious and unswerving faith in what appeared to them to be essential, they were continually moving on from one new point of view to another, giving up what had seemed to them established knowledge, and again and again reviewing and questioning themselves and their work.

At this point it is fitting to recall the magnificent audacity with which Freud, alone and unsupported, undertook a self-analysis and discovered all the contents of the personal unconscious, from the Oedipus complex to infantile sexuality, which have today become common knowledge for Western man. A man of Freud's type, his whole outlook based on his conviction of the supreme value of consciousness, needed the extraordinary courage and uncompromising vision of the explorer, as well as his unremitting tenacity, not only to discover the fact of resistance—his own resistance—to the contents of the unconscious, but also to break through to the contents from which this resistance tried to distract him.

Yet, just as we realize the unequaled originality of this effort, we come up against the problem of what Jung has called the "personal equation" of man, that is, the specific stamp of the individual with all his natural one-sidedness. An awareness of this personal equation, however, presupposes an analysis in which a second person, of a different temperament and different background, confronts, as an incorruptible opposite, the one-sidedness and the blind spots of the analysand, and so brings them to consciousness and dissolves them. With all due admiration for the creative achievement of

Freud's self-analysis, one still cannot doubt that, even in the case of such a genius, it must fail to yield the same result as the dialogue of a normal analysis. The movement to and fro which, in the form of the phenomenon of the transference, provides the central core of every analysis, is lacking in a self-analysis, as Jones himself has pointed out. When, however, this dynamic experience of the "thou" as essentially "other" is lacking, the unconscious data of the personal equation must remain for the most part uncorrected and the loneliness of the unconscious prejudice is not dissolved.

That Freud was in this sense unanalyzed has long been known. It is, however, surprising and at the same time disturbing that the same applies to all Freud's "paladins," who by the solemn bestowal of a ring were confirmed as members of the innermost circle and therewith as leaders of the psychoanalytic movement.[2] Apart from those on the periphery of the movement, all these men except Jones (Ferenczi, Abraham, Sachs, and Eitingon) were Jews. This brings us to a problem that belongs both to Freud and to psychoanalysis, namely the Jewish problem, the significance of which has not yet been given enough attention and which in this context can only be hinted at.

By this we do not mean the problems arising in this Jewish group from anti-Semitism and deep-seated resentment, for these are relatively comprehensible, and

2. Jones, II, p. 161/182. It may be noted in passing that the analysis of the only one "analyzed," Jones, does not correspond to anything called analysis today. [Further references are to vol. II of Jones.]

were characteristic of unanalyzed Jews of the "assimilation period" and long after it. Often enough the Jew instinctively feels the "goy" to be the enemy and the anti-Semite, even when he allows himself to behave anti-Semitically. The Jewish problem of Freud and his paladins is much deeper and by no means a mere negative bias but a precondition, essentially related to Freud's great work and to psychoanalysis itself. That Freud was indeed conscious of his specifically Jewish qualities is clear from a passage advising Ferenczi how to reply to Maeder, who felt that, in the conflict between the Viennese (Freud) and the Zurich (Bleuler-Jung) schools, the difference between the Jews (Vienna) and the non-Jews (Zurich) was significant. Freud wrote: "Certainly there are great differences between the Jewish and Aryan spirit. We can observe that every day. Hence there would assuredly be here and there differences in outlook on life and art" (p. 149/168). This statement is, in its simple matter-of-factness, so significant because, when expressed by a non-Jew, e.g. Jung, it has always been foolishly taken as a proof of anti-Semitism. With equal simplicity and as much justification, Freud then, however, goes on to state: "But there should not be such a thing as Aryan or Jewish science. Results in science must be identical, though the presentation of them may vary. If these differences mirror themselves in the apprehension of objective relationships in science there must be something wrong."

Our distance from the conflicts of this creative period, during which Freud and Jung came to the parting of the ways, enables us to see that what Freud took for granted as "scientific" was partly colored by his own unconscious prejudices which had never been analyzed. It almost looks as if he was unaware of this when he wrote to Abraham: "Don't forget that really it is easier for you to follow my thoughts than for Jung, since to begin with you are completely independent and then racial relationship brings you closer to my intellectual constitution" (p. 48/53). One can gather from this sentence that to be a Jew was, in a way, a better "racial" preparation for a scientific approach to psychology. This statement, like nearly all statements about fundamental racial characteristics, shows an unconscious prejudice. We find this confirmed in the whole of Freud's work, where the chief distinction is seen to lie in the fact that, in contrast to the Jews, non-Jews regard religious contents as of essential significance. It is typical that the word "mystical" is used to mean "of religious content," and one hardly trusts one's eyes when in this context one reads Freud's statement: "We Jews have an easier time, having no mystical element" (p. 49/55).

This fundamental unconsciousness of Freud the Jew about his own historical, if not personal, foundation constitutes a "complex" typical of this whole group. It shows itself positively as well as negatively in Freud's work, because a complex functions in the unconscious as a dynamic factor. Just as Freud "forgets" that the Jews are the religious people par excellence and have, in the kabbala and in Hasidism, produced the most important mystical ideas and movements, so he never took serious account of the deeper transpersonal levels of the unconscious that are at work behind the merely per-

sonal unconscious. The' antireligious affect is characteristic of a large number of creatively gifted Jews of
the nineteenth century, that is, of the assimilation period; it is an expression of the liberation—absolutely
necessary both historically and for the individual—from
the yoke of Jewish orthodoxy that took place under the
aegis of the Enlightenment and the (extremely onesided) development of the natural sciences. The clearest
and most naive expression of this view is given by
Ferenczi in the following words: "It has seldom been
so clear to me as now what a psychological advantage
it signifies to be born a Jew and to have been spared in
one's childhood all the *atavistic nonsense*" (p. 153/173;
E.N.'s italics).

This was how the unconscious premises of the Jewish
group of analysts came into conflict with the completely
different character of the non-Jews, whose historical
background produced no such antireligious affect and
for whom (e.g. for Jung and for many others) it was
impossible to dismiss the old religious phenomena as
mere "atavistic nonsense," although this positivistic attitude was widespread and fashionable around the turn
of the century. If we now point out some Jewish traits
in Freud, which were conditioned by his time, and
some of his personal "complexes," it must be clearly understood that these unconscious characteristics did not
prevent a genius like Freud from reaching beyond the
purely personal and achieving something of relatively
general validity. The universal principle that he discovered, and for which discovery his unconscious Jewish antireligious affect was partly responsible, was the

psychic significance of the father image (the patriarchate) for Western man.

It has long been evident that for Freud the "father complex" played a decisive role. Yet it would be wrong to understand this complex merely as a matter of individual and family history. Close behind it, without Freud's ever having been conscious of this, stands the confrontation with the Jewish Father-God, that is, psychologically, with the father archetype.

Two characteristic incidents from Freud's life that Jones mentions in his biography should be cited (vol. I, p. 317/348; vol. II, p. 146/165ff.), as they shed light on the problem of how closely the contents of the personal unconscious, the relation of child to father, brother, etc., are connected with the attitude toward transpersonal contents. On both occasions, when Freud suddenly fainted, it happened in connection with his pupil and friend Jung, who later parted from him. The first time Freud fainted was after he had succeeded in converting Jung from his antialcoholism.[3] Freud himself interpreted this as a "failure in the face of success." He paid for his "victory" over Jung with his fainting; but this happened because Freud, according to his own interpretation, identified Jung with his "younger brother," for whose death he had as a child wished out of jealousy, like every older sibling. When, however, this brother actually died in childhood, this naturally led to anxiety and feelings of

3. [Jung, not originally an abstainer, had become one under the influence of Eugen Bleuler, his chief at the Burghölzli Clinic. Freud persuaded him to drink wine at dinner at Bremen on Aug. 20, 1909, on the eve of their departure for the United States.]

guilt on the part of the elder brother about his "victory."

The second occasion of Freud's fainting is no less significant and is closely connected with the first.[4] A conversation took place in which Jung—wrongly, we think—denied Freud's thesis of the general occurrence of death wishes toward parents. There followed a discussion about the great Egyptian king Ikhnaton. Freud remarked that this was the king who erased his father's name from all monuments, and Jung replied that Freud had overemphasized this relation to the father and that the most important act of this king had been the establishment of monotheism—whereupon Freud fainted. The real issue here is deeper than the merely personal problem of Freud's identification with the annihilated father and Jung's with the annihilating son, although this constellation also has its validity. Beyond this, however, the philosophical and psychic differences between the two men become apparent. Whereas Freud only acknowledges the personal father and is aware of nothing transpersonal, nothing beyond this affect-relationship, Jung stresses the significance of the transpersonal father image that exists independently of the personal relation to the father.

For Freud the killing of the father is not only a childhood incident of the Oedipus complex. It is well known that in his ethnologically untenable work, *Totem and*

4. [For Jung's account (which had not been written when Neumann composed the present essay) see *Memories, Dreams, Reflections*, p. 157/153. The occasion was a meeting of the leaders of the International Psychoanalytic Association in Munich on Nov. 24, 1912, to discuss Association business. See *The Freud/Jung Letters*, pp. 520-22.]

Taboo,[5] he made the allegedly primeval killing of the
father into the origin of religion and supposed the Father-God to be nothing but a glorification of the murdered tribal father. It is symptomatic that Freud wrote
this work at the time of his emotional reaction over
Jung's withdrawal, and emphasized on May 8, 1913: "I
am working on the last section of the *Totem* which
comes at the right moment to deepen the gap [between
him and Jung] by fathoms" (p. 353/397). He thought
the essay "would serve to make a sharp division between us and all Aryan religiosity. For that will be the
result of it. . . . In the dispute with Zurich it comes at
the right time to divide us as an acid does a salt."

It is doubtful whether this clearly expressed affect can
ever form the basis of a science, and one remembers
Freud's own words: "If these differences mirror themselves in the apprehension of objective relationships in
science, there must be something wrong" (p. 149/168).
Freud was in a mood of elation while he was writing
this work, but later he was assailed by doubts. Ferenczi
and Jones interpreted these as follows: "his elation represented the excitement of killing and eating the father
and . . . his doubts were only the reaction" (p. 354/397).
This interpretation was accepted by Freud and elaborat-
ed in the statement: "Then [in *The Interpretation of
Dreams*] I described the wish to kill one's father, and
now I have been describing the actual killing; after all
it is a big step from a wish to a deed." It is noteworthy

5. [Originally published 1912/1913. In Standard Edn., vol.
XIII.]

that Freud talks of the deed as if he had committed and not described it.

But Freud's magnificent battle with the unconscious Jewish problem of the Father and the Father-God goes on. Simultaneously with his *On the History of the Psychoanalytic Movement*, in which he rid himself of his anger over the desertion of his pupils, he writes the essay on "The Moses of Michelangelo."[6] In it he interprets the figure of Moses as an expression of the great effort Moses had to make to control his anger when he saw God and himself deserted by the people. It has not escaped the attention of his pupils that Freud was, on the one hand, identified with the father figure, namely Moses[7] (as was already clear from the Ikhnaton incident), and on the other hand, opposed the father, as son. This tragic unconscious dichotomy forced Freud to publish the study on the Moses of Michelangelo anonymously and to justify this by saying, "Why disgrace Moses by putting my name to it?" (p. 366/410); it also caused him, in his last book, to make Moses an Egyptian. In a similar way, the figure of the Jewish-Christian Father-God, killed in *Totem and Taboo* and in *The Future of an Illusion*,[8] is resurrected in the human psyche as the "superego" and continues to play there the same violent and repressive part of the moral lawgiver, against whom the rebellious patricide of the lib-

6. [Both works originally published 1914. The former is in vol. xiv, the latter in vol. xiii, of the Standard Edn.]

7. Cf. Jones, vol. ii, p. 33/37.

8. [Originally published 1927; in Standard Edn., vol. xxi.]

erating Jewish sons had originally—and rightly—been directed.

Freud's heroic struggle with the father archetype of Judaism within him is one that plays an essential part in the changes taking place in modern Judaism. Judaism has broken its old religious fetters without having as yet arrived at a new orientation. This battle is not Freud's personal affair only, nor is it simply a problem of Jewry itself; Western culture (religion, society, and morals) is mainly formed by this father image and the psychic structure of the individual is partly damaged by it. It is for this reason that Freud's findings, his deductions and documentations connected with the Oedipus complex and patricide, are of the greatest importance and relatively true as applied to people living in the patriarchal world. Patriarchal culture means the culture of consciousness and the rule of reason. Today, as always, the battle of Western consciousness is fought in the spirit of the Old Testament war against the Mother-Goddess. It is fascinating to observe how Freud, hesitantly, reluctantly, and forced by his own integrity, leaves the territory of the holy Father-God who sanctifies consciousness and moves toward confrontation with the "other side," the unconscious.

Yet, although he went so far as to realize the necessity of "patricide" and, at the end of his life, abandoned the monistic and monotheistic attitude that he had originally maintained against Jung, the Jewish taboo of the Mother-Goddess, that is, of the unconscious, prevailed with him to the end. Just as the medieval Jew characteristically (and, strangely enough, also the kabbala) connected the masculine with grace and the feminine with judgment and evil—compare the merciful figure of the Madonna in Christianity—so Freud sees the unconscious as an "id," generally hostile to culture and to consciousness and always an overpowering negative. Freud's inherent honesty made him admit that in the picture of human history which he—wrongly—drew in *Totem and Taboo*, the figure of the Mother-Goddess who preceded the Father-God had been lacking. He never discovered the decisive significance of the mother in the destiny of the individual and of mankind. His psychology of the feminine is therefore a patriarchal misconception and his lack of understanding of the nature of religion and of artistic creation comes from the same unawareness of the creative psyche which, mythologically, is connected with the Mother-Goddess and the prepatriarchal level of the unconscious.

As a great Jew at the turning point not only of the patriarchal era but also of the cultural history of the Jews, Freud opened the way for the liberation of man from the oppression of the old father figure to which he himself remained deeply fixated. Like his great forebear Moses, he led the way out of servitude, but the land of promise, in which the earth mother has a place beside the celestial father, he saw only from afar.

V

C. G. JUNG: 1955

On July 26, the greatest psychologist of our time, C. G. Jung, will be eighty years old. Although Jung's significance is still keenly debated, the influence of his work all over the world and in many cultural fields outside psychology—for example, in poetry, literary criticism, anthropology, mythology, etc.—is steadily increasing. To anyone who is fully acquainted with Jung's work and has followed its development at close quarters during the last few decades, it will be obvious that the whole corpus of his later writings has scarcely begun to make its impact and that it still really belongs to the future. To some extent, this is due to the fact that Jung's scientific investigations have never lost their dynamic character. With the spirit of an authentic revolutionary pioneer he has never ceased to make new and startling discoveries and gains throughout the varied phases of his career. Public acceptance of his work has therefore inevitably lagged behind.

You would not make yourself particularly popular with Jung if you were to tell him that he is a revolutionary. His conscious outlook in fact betrays a certain

"C. G. Jung: Zum 80. Geburtstag," *Merkur* (Stuttgart), no. 89 (July 1955).

tendency towards conservatism. For example, he regards
Nature herself as essentially a conservative force, so
that to be rooted in nature is equivalent to being linked
with the world of the ancestors and of the origins of
things. He thinks and feels in terms of natural relationships, just as he himself is linked personally with the
Swiss landscape and with his tower on Lake Zurich.

However, these obvious and basic traits must not
blind us to the fact that, as we now know, Nature—in
spite of what used to be said about her—is actually very
fond of leaping, and one of her leaps is Jung himself. It
is true that, in such a leap as this, Nature overcomes
nature and reveals herself to us with a transparency we
have never seen before. However, for the man who
represents this leap in his own person, the process of
learning to tolerate himself and of coming to terms with
his own nature and with nature herself in general is a
painful and arduous undertaking. It is only by continually questioning himself and the nature which he sees
around him that such a man may finally acquire the
ability to affirm himself in his own essential being.

In Jung's case, we certainly gain the impression that
he is constantly returning to nature, that he is passionately opposed to any kind of speculation, and that he is
never tired of protesting that he is an empiricist. He is
an empiricist, in fact, for he thinks nothing out for himself, yet at the same time, in a curious way he fails to
recognize his own true quality and is all too easily inclined to forget that the experience on which he bases
his empiricism is nothing humdrum or commonplace,
but that in scope and content it transcends the experi-

ence of his contemporaries to a quite extraordinary degree. It is for this reason that they regard it as "mystical" and will inevitably continue to see it in that light until they themselves graduate to that experience of a larger reality which is beyond their ken at the present time.

When Jung, as a young psychiatrist, joined forces with Freud in 1908 (during the period when Freud was still being ostracized) and became the leader of the international psychoanalytical movement, he was as far ahead of his time and his colleagues as he was five years later, when he parted company with Freud. We can only really understand the loneliness into which his path then led him, and to what extent—as the future will emphasize—he was to blaze new and unexplored trails for Western man, if we realize that today, more than forty years later, the view of the world held by the professional psychoanalysts and psychiatrists, who are still, by and large, very satisfied with themselves, roughly corresponds to the stage Jung left behind him in 1912. This was in fact the stage represented by personalistic depth psychology, which follows the destiny of the individual in the context of the events of his personal development and seeks to clarify and to change it by so doing.

The next leap, if that is the right word for a process that has been brewing for a long time and then suddenly bursts upon the discoverer with the abruptness of an invasion which forces him to mobilize every ounce of his powers, was the discovery of the collective unconscious, or in other words, of an unconscious psychic structure which is common to the entire human race. This discovery, which Freud first became aware of in his late work *Moses and Monotheism*, and which is now gaining acceptance throughout the world of psycho-analysis in the form of the theory of "great" parental figures, finally shattered the narrow framework of an existence conceived of in purely bourgeois family terms.

What now emerged was the primal psychic world of mankind, the world of mythology, the world of primitive man and of all those myriad forms of religion and art in which man is visibly gripped and carried away by the suprapersonal power that sustains and nourishes all creative development. The human psyche stood revealed as a creative force in the here and now which plays a vital role as a source of meaning and synthesis in all sorts of diseases and in ongoing healing processes of every kind.

There is nothing mystical or complicated about those primordial images of the psyche that are known as archetypes. They are an expression of the simple fact that every human being comes into the world equipped not only with a typically human body and nervous system but with a psychic apparatus which is no less distinctive and characteristic of the human species. And just as every human being—in contradistinction to other forms of life—sees and hears in a typically human fashion, so too the way in which he experiences and interprets the world is decisively affected from the outset by the primordial images of the human psyche. These inner images are projected in experience, which means that they appear to primitive man, to children, and also largely to so-called modern man as "outer," not as inner, realities. Among these "dominant" inner archetypal images are to be found Father and Mother, Lover and Beloved, Hero, Wise Man, and many others. An archetype of this kind, such as, e.g., the image of the Great Mother, which in the history of civilization appears as a goddess, is normally triggered off by the experience of the personal mother, but the same primordial image is constitutionally present in every human being and frequently takes its course quite independently of the person who has triggered it off. For example, the cause of an illness in a given subject may be the "Terrible Mother," even if the subject's personal mother was by no means terrible; on the other hand, a poet may have a lifelong relationship with the Good Mother although his personal mother may have been insignificant and even apparently "negative."

The significance of such archetypal images can scarcely be exaggerated. Archetypal dominants have played a vital if not a decisive role, not only in religion and art and so in the cultural life of mankind, but also in the psychic life (both normal and pathological) of human beings in all ages and of all nations.

The significance of Jung's next basic discovery has remained largely unrecognized for historical reasons, since it is closely bound up with the complicated texts and images of medieval alchemy. Jung recognized both the possibility and the existence of a process of transformation within the personality in which the personal and the transpersonal layers and structures of the psyche both play an essential part. In an age of increasing collectivization, the historical significance of this discovery is really to be found in the *rediscovery* of the individual as an essential nucleus of creative activity in human civilization. A collective attitude that regarded the psychological development of the individual almost as an individualistic vice and the agreement of the individual with the recognized collective values of the period as the highest and indeed the only imperative is here confronted by the revolutionary counterposition, which insists that a sound collective ordering of society is only possible when the individual is at liberty to realize his own inner creative freedom.

In the course of his research into the collective unconscious, which occupied a period of several decades, Jung did more than rediscover the world of primitive man as an essential part of the total personality. He encountered the ultimate foundation of the psyche itself, which in spite of all typological differences is the common ground between Western and Eastern man; and in so doing he created the basis for a new humanism.

In an epoch in which a psychological preoccupation with those religious phenomena that have always stirred mankind to its depths has been mistakenly identified with mysticism, Jung has attempted to lay bare the universal psychic substrate which underlies Indian, Chinese, and Islamic texts, Gnostic and alchemical symbolism, and the dogma of the Catholic Church—that substrate by whose dynamism, whether consciously or unconsciously, the human race is ultimately motivated.

The record as I have described it so far would be sufficient in itself to constitute the supreme achievement of a creative lifetime. Jung, however, was not content to rest on his laurels. In his *Answer to Job* (written when he was over 75), he struck a blow, which is still almost completely misunderstood, against the canon of the entire Western religious establishment. In a spirit of the profoundest religious compassion, harrowed by the evil and misery in the world, Jung leveled an accusation against the old divine image of the God of righteousness and wrath, which still survives in Christian consciousness in the form of the God of the Old Testament. He "calls God to witness against God," with the same justification as Abraham and Moses when they strove to defend themselves against God's arbitrary vengefulness.

There is indeed a justification for such a revolutionary act. It is not, however, to be found in theological scholarship, nor in some well-thought-out philosophical or scientific viewpoint, but rather in a justly merited claim to represent humanity against the suprapersonal powers.

Anyone who has spent a lifetime in contact with human beings and has consistently championed their interests has earned the right to represent their cause before— and against!—God.

There are two Hasidic stories that have always seemed to me to typify this kind of Jungian "vis-à-vis." One says, we should always behave as if in every human being we speak to we are encountering God himself. The other requires of us that whenever we are confronted with a fellow mortal in need, we should act as if there were no God and we were alone in all the world with that particular person. In real life, it is of course axiomatic that no one can possibly fulfill these demands. Yet the fact that Jung comes so close to doing so—closer than any other human being I know—confirms his right as I see it to represent suffering humanity before God, as he does in his *Answer to Job.*

It is scarcely to be expected that our contemporaries, who are usually without a clue, should understand what is really involved in resistance to this old God-image and in the passionate championing of a new, hitherto unknown manifestation of the godhead who continually reveals himself anew. But there are many people who are at least capable of grasping the fact that the increasing "lack of religion" of modern man is really no more than an unconscious process of *turning away* from the image of a God of righteousness which has lost all credibility and from the affect-laden, chauvinistic "love" of this God and *towards* a humanity which has been called upon to suffer beyond measure. That Jung still possessed the strength and courage, in spite of his old age and of the perennial *misconception* of him as a mystic, to incur the odium of a new and diametrically opposite misconception of him as an atheist, is the most convincing proof of the inexhaustible, revolutionary power of his genius and of the profound seriousness of his sense of responsibility.

The most recent "leap" taken by the man who is eighty years old this year is also entirely characteristic of him. Although ostensibly unrelated to *Answer to Job*, it actually illustrates Jung's inability to let anything apparently "negative," such as his accusation against the God of Job, stand without some reference to something positive. The paper "Synchronicity: An Acausal Connecting Principle" is a scientific attempt to extend modern man's view of the world by including in it the discovery that certain "chance events" which are "acausally" or "noncausally" connected with each other are actually meaningful factors that belong essentially to the totality of the world. This problem, which at first appears so remote and unintelligible, will prove to be of the greatest significance for modern man's future view of the world. If the premise of synchronicity, to which Jung's paper is a tentative contribution, can be validated, this would mean no more nor less than that phenomena which have hitherto been described in theological terms as "miracles" are in principle contained in the structure of our world.

It is typical of the quality of Jung's genius that in extreme old age, when he was already in a sense beyond the good and evil represented by the moral judgment of his contemporaries, he dared not merely to shake the foundations of the traditional Christian image of God, but to open up at the same time a new and illuminating approach to the possibility of religious experience for modern man. Jung's research has plainly shown that the concept of the self as the center of the self-regulating system of the psyche points beyond the purely psychic dimension. But the implications go further than that. The world in its turn produces certain strange and un-canny phenomena which, though acausal and scarcely definable in rational terms, are nevertheless observable events that tend to recur in certain contexts; such phe-nomena reveal a secret dimension of order and meaning which encroaches on the sphere of the human psyche.

It is still far too early for Jung's contemporaries to ap-preciate the full scope of his significance. We live in an age of ever-increasing specialization. Knowledge is subdivided into the most minute compartments, within which more and more material is accumulated with antlike assiduity. This piling up of material goes hand in in hand with a narrowing of mental horizons, as the distance which separates speciality from speciality and province from province steadily widens. On the other hand, world developments in our time, in spite of political splits and iron curtains, are moving in the direction of a universal humanism; the unity of mankind is becoming more and more obvious. Not only has C. G. Jung laid the scientific foundation for our understanding of the essential unity of human nature and human culture; he is also the first representative of a new type of humanity that unites East and West, the very modern and the primitive, science and religion, the collective and the altogether individual, in the universality of a single person.

C. G. Jung is the only really great man I have met in my life. As teacher and friend for more than three decades, he has constantly provided me with new and vital substance for both love and vexation—like Nature herself, the lover of leaping, the superior of man. And when, in this man with all his weaknesses and all his greatness, I struck upon that which is greater than man, yet in which all human qualities are grounded—that was for me a decisive and profoundly orientative experience.

The most important thing about my encounter with Jung was not what I learned from him about myself, mankind, and the world—though without all this my life as it is would be inconceivable. Jung's spontaneity was such that he would often at first sight give the impression he had misunderstood me or that we were talking at cross-purposes. But what appeared to be his unrelated way of letting himself go and speaking about himself and the world in general was actually related to his vis-à-vis on a deeper level than could have been achieved by any willed effort of the head or the heart by themselves. Subsequently, often years later, it would dawn upon me how essentially right he had been, and how he had bypassed my ego, as it were, and had spoken directly to the center of my psyche. This utmost in relatedness, which so many people have experienced in Jung, is to my mind proof positive of the dynamic impact of his wholeness, working as it did beyond the range of his knowledge and of all purely rational understanding. If, against the background of his social environment, he often has the effect of a giant among dwarfs, who always has to stoop a little to make himself understood, this is only another way of saying that his real vis-à-vis is only to be found where man in his wholeness listens and responds. It was in this way, when I came to him as a young man, that he gave me, like a gift from a higher power, the courage to be myself. And later, too, when if he had been a lesser man differences in temperament and in circumstances would long ago have created misunderstandings between us, he remained—though at times closer and at times further away—always a central vis-à-vis in my life. For all these things, now as ever, I owe him the profoundest gratitude.

INDEX

INDEX

Aaron, 128-9
Abraham, 120-1, 252
Abraham, K., 236, 238
Adam, 117-8, 121
Advocate Huld, 46-8, 53-5,
  58-9, 61, 66-9, 71, 75, 79
alchemy, 250
anima, 139, 200-203, 206;
  -image, sister as carrier of,
  205; -image and mother,
  140; negative, 204n
anti-Semitism, 236-7
Apollo, 198
archetype(s), 249-50
Artemis, 198
artist(s), 203-7, 214-5; relationship to mother and
  sister, 205

Baal Shem Tov, I., 133n
Bathsheba, 114
Beatrice, 206
Beethoven, Ludwig van,
  204, 206
Benjamin, 124-5
Bible, 113-37
Bleuler, E., 237, 240n
Block, 45-6, 48, 59-60, 63-6,
  69-70, 73-5
Bluebeard motif, 167-170,
  180
"bread and wine," symbol-

ism of, in Trakl's poetry,
  158-61
bridegroom and bride, symbolism of, 136-7
Bürstner, Fräulein, 5, 13,
  23, 25, 35, 50, 108-9
Buschbeck, E., 149-50

cabala/kabbala, 134, 238,
  244
Cathedral, 76-80, 89, 107
Catholic elements, 180
causality, 77-9
Chagall, Marc, and the
  Bible, 113-37; *The Call of
  Moses at the Burning
  Bush*, 126; *The Discovery
  of the Infant Moses by the
  Princess*, 126; plate depicting the promise of
  future blessedness to
  Jerusalem, 136-7; plate
  illustrating meeting of
  Elijah and the widow, 133
chaplain, 77-8, 80, 82, 85-6,
  88-90, 92, 94-5, 99, 103,
  107-8
child, divine, 126
childhood, 210-14, 217
Christ, 119, 156, 180
complex, father-, 240
confession, 87-9, 100

259

"Leonardo da Vinci and
the Mother Archetype,"
206*n*; "Man and Trans-
formation," 157*n*, 215*n*;
"The Moon and Matri-
archal Consciousness,"
168*n*; "Narcissism, Nor-
mal Self-Formation . . . ,"
203*n*, 214*n*; "On Mozart's
Magic Flute," 217*n*,
229*n*; *The Origins and
History of Conscious-
ness*, 125*n*, 138*n*, 195*n*,
197*n*, 200*n*, 204*n*; *The
Place of Creation*, 208*n*
Nietzsche, F. W., 148, 184
Noah, 121

objective psyche, 36-40, 56,
72
Oedipus complex, 235, 241,
244

Pharaoh, 121-2, 124, 128
psychoanalysis, 232

Rank, O., 204
Rembrandt, 115-6, 134; *The
Return of the Prodigal
Son*, 125

Sachs, H., 236
sacrifice, 28-9
salvation, 135
Samuel, 122
Satan, 171, 216
Saul, 121
Scholem, G., 133*n*

self, 211, 217, 254
self-consciousness, 57
sexuality, infantile, 235
shadow, 184
Sheba, Queen of, 123
sin, original, 167
sister, archetype, 206, 209-
10, 221; brother's rela-
tionship with, 197-203,
209
Solomon, 121-3
soul-image, 201-2
spirit, divine, 118
Spoerri, T., 142-4, 146-7,
149, 210*n*, 215*n*
Suffering Servant, 114
superego, 243
Susannah, 114
synchronicity, 253-4

Tables, breaking of, 129
Titorelli, 46, 50, 54, 59, 61,
67, 81, 84
Trakl, G., 138-231; alienation, 158-9; and drugs,
145-6; and his father,
146-7; craving for death,
144-5; death, 151; his narcissism, 149; incest with
sister, 138-9, 147-8, 163,
171, 175, 179-80, 193-4,
208, 210, 212, 215-6; relationship with mother,
138-9, 144, 146-8, 173,
175, 195, 215-6; POETRY:
The Accursed, 174;
"Autumn night, so cool,
advances," 222; *The Beau-*

GPSR Authorized Representative: Easy Access System Europe - Mustamäe tee 50, 10621 Tallinn, Estonia, gpsr.requests@easproject.com